Jeff Bridges is _{an Academy Award winning actor,} song-
writer and _{photographer. He is a founder of the} End
Hunger Network and the national spokesman for Share
Our Strength's No Kid Hungry campaign.

Bernie Glassman founded the Zen Community of
New York, which later became Zen Peacemakers, an
international order of social activists. A longtime Zen
teacher, he also founded the Greyston Mandala, a network of for-profit and not-for-profit entities creating
jobs, housing and programmes to support individuals
and their families on the path to self-sufficiency.

JEFFBRIDGES.COM

ZENPEACEMAKERS.ORG

THE DUDE AND THE ZEN MASTER

THE DUDE AND THE ZEN MASTER

JEFF BRIDGES & BERNIE GLASSMAN

CORGI BOOKS

TRANSWORLD PUBLISHERS
61–63 Uxbridge Road, London W5 5SA
A Random House Group Company
www.transworldbooks.co.uk

THE DUDE AND THE ZEN MASTER
A CORGI BOOK: 9780552169554

First published in Great Britain
in 2013 by Bantam Press
an imprint of Transworld Publishers
Corgi edition published 2014

Photographs on title page, 11, 57, 121 and 213 by Alan Kozlowski
Photograph on page 81 by Jeff Bridges
Book design by Claire Naylon Vaccaro

Jeff Bridges and Bernie Glassman have asserted their right under the Copyright,
Designs and Patents Act 1988 to be identified as the authors of this work.

A CIP catalogue record for this book
is available from the British Library.

Addresses for Random House Group Ltd companies outside the UK
can be found at: www.randomhouse.co.uk
The Random House Group Ltd Reg. No. 954009

The Random House Group Limited supports the Forest Stewardship Council®
(FSC®), the leading international forest-certification organisation. Our books
carrying the FSC label are printed on FSC®-certified paper. FSC is the only
forest-certification scheme supported by the leading environmental
organisations, including Greenpeace. Our paper procurement policy
can be found at www.randomhouse.co.uk/environment

Typeset in 12/19pt Walbaum
Printed and bound by CPI Group (UK) Ltd, Croydon, CR0 4YY.

2 4 6 8 10 9 7 5 3 1

To all the hungry spirits

CONTENTS

JUST THROW THE FU**ING BALL, MAN!

THE DUDE ABIDES *AND*
THE DUDE IS NOT IN

THAT RUG REALLY TIED
THE ROOM TOGETHER,
DID IT NOT?

ENJOYIN' MY COFFEE

JEFF'S INTRODUCTION

So . . . my buddy Bernie Glassman says to me one day, "Did you know that the Dude in *The Big Lebowski* is considered by many Buddhists to be a Zen master?"

I said, "What the fuck are you talkin' 'bout, man?"

He said, "Oh yeah."

I said, "You gotta be kidding. We never talked about Zen or Buddhism while we were making *Lebowski*. The brothers* never said anything about that."

---

* Ethan and Joel Coen wrote and directed *The Big Lebowski*, released in 1998.

"Yeah," laughed Bernie, "just look at their name—the Koan brothers."

Koans are Zen stories that only make sense if you can see that life and reality are different from your opinions about them. Most of the famous ones were written in China a long time ago.

Bernie went on: "*The Big Lebowski* is filled with koans, only they're in the 'parlance of our time,' to quote the Dude."

"What are you talkin' about, man? What do you mean?" I asked him.

"It's filled with 'em, like: *The Dude abides*—very Zen, man; or *The Dude is not in*—classic Zen; or *Donny, you're out of your element*, or *That rug really tied the room together*. It's loaded with 'em."

"Really?" I said.

Now, my buddy Bernie is a Zen master himself. In the early sixties he left his job as an aeronautical engineer at McDonnell Douglas to study at the Zen Center of Los Angeles with his teacher, Maezumi Roshi, a great Japanese master who helped bring Zen to this country. Bernie became one of the first American teachers. He not only started the Zen Peacemakers, he also built homes for homeless families, child-care centers, housing and medical treatment for folks with AIDS, and companies—including a big bakery—to hire people who didn't have jobs. That bakery won an award one year for best New York cheesecake and now makes brownie products for Ben & Jerry's Ice Cream. He's considered a major player in socially engaged Buddhism around the world.

I met Bernie at a dinner thrown by a neighbor of mine for him and Ram Dass, author of *Be Here Now* and many other wonderful books. I sat between these two guys and had a great time. Bernie and I really hit it off; we both cared about a lot of the same stuff.

This is where *Lebowski* comes in. Bernie has been interested for some time now in making Zen more accessible to our times and culture, relevant and down-to-earth, and he felt that *Lebowski* did that big-time. So he asked me if I wanted to write a book about that.

I said, "Okay."

So here's what we did. We went up to my ranch in Montana with our fellow jamster, Alan Kozlowski, and jammed for five days. Alan was the photographer/recorder cat; he recorded our dialogue, took pictures, gave his opinions, etc. After that we went home. Bernie's wife, Eve, started working with the transcripts. We met some more, hung out on the phone and on Skype, tweaked some things, and . . . here it is.

To me, this book is sort of like a snakeskin. A snakeskin is something you might find on the side of the road and make something out of—a belt, say, or a hatband. The snake itself heads off doing more snake stuff—getting it on with lady snakes, eating rats, making more snakeskins, et cetera.

I look at movies the same way. The final movie is the snakeskin, which can be pretty interesting and valuable. The snake is what happens while we're making the movie—the relationships, the experience. I try to open wide and get really connected with the people I'm working with—the director, the cast, the production crew—all of us cooking in a safe and generous space, trying to get the job done. And we have to get that fire going as soon as we can, because our time together is finite, two or three months, maybe six. That's all the time we've got to come up with what we intend. Or, every once in a wonderful while, with something that transcends all our desires and intentions. I love it when that happens, and it does quite often because of all the unknowns involved. I think that's why I'm still making movies.

The actual "snake" of this book was the hang, the jam, with Bernie, Eve, Alan, and everyone else who helped. It was the chance to dance, create, be intimate, and be free.

So, here it is. Hope you dig it.

Hope's interesting, isn't it? I can't turn hope off, it's hopeless.

Jeff Bridges, *Santa Barbara, California*

BERNIE'S INTRODUCTION

All my life I've been interested in expressing my truth in ways that almost anyone can understand. A famous Japanese Zen master, Hakuun Yasutani Roshi, said that unless you can explain Zen in words that a fisherman will comprehend, you don't know what you're talking about. Some fifty years ago a UCLA professor told me the same thing about applied mathematics. We like to hide from the truth behind foreign-sounding words or mathematical lingo. There's a saying: *The truth is always encountered but rarely perceived.* If we don't perceive it, we can't help ourselves and we can't much help anyone else.

I met the Dude on DVD sometime in the late 1990s. A few years later I met Jeff Bridges in Santa Barbara and we started hanging, as he likes to put it, often while smoking cigars. Jeff has done movies from an early age; less known, but almost as long-standing, is his commitment to ending world hunger. I was an aeronautical engineer and mathematician in my early years, but mostly I've taught Zen Buddhism, and that's where we both met. Not just in meditation, which is what most people think of when they hear Zen, but the Zen of action, of living freely in the world without causing harm, of relieving our own suffering and the suffering of others.

We soon discovered that we would often be joined by another shadowy figure, somebody called the Dude. We both liked his way of putting things and it's fun to learn from someone you can't see. Only his words were so pithy they needed more expounding; hence, this book.

May it meet with his approval, and may it benefit all beings.

Bernie Glassman, *Montague, Massachusetts*

JUST THROW
THE FU**ING BALL, MAN!

I.

SOMETIMES YOU EAT

THE BEAR, AND SOMETIMES,

WELL, HE EATS YOU

JEFF: We're making the movie *The Big Lebowski*, and everyone who's seen the movie knows that the Dude and Walter dig bowling, right? Now, I've bowled a little bit in the past, but I'm not an expert like the Dude. So the Coen brothers hire a master bowler to teach John Goodman, Steve Buscemi, and me how to bowl. The master bowler is a world champion and he brings his assistant along.

I ask the bowling master, "How do you think the Dude might bowl? Does he prepare for a long time? Does he have to get his mind set? Is he like Art Carney in *The Honeymooners*?" Whenever Art Carney would be asked to sign something, say a document, Jackie Gleason would tell him, "Sign there, Norton," and Carney would start twitching and fidgeting, carrying on for so long that Gleason would finally yell, "SIGN THE DOCUMENT!" So I ask the bowling master if the Dude might be like that.

His assistant starts laughing so hard he just about pees in his pants. The master bowler shakes his head and rolls his eyes, looking embarrassed, so I ask him what's going on.

"Oh, nothing, nothing," the assistant says.

The master says, "Go on, you can tell him."

The assistant says, "No, you tell him."

Finally the master tells his story. It seems that years ago he tried to bowl like in the book *Zen in the Art of Archery*. That book teaches the student to completely let go of his ego in order to hit the bull's-eye. If the mind is settled and clear, the pins are practically down before the bowler cocks his hand back to throw the ball. So the bowling master tried to get into that mind-set and ended up like Art Carney. He had certain tics to release tension in his body and he'd do this little stress-relieving dance that would go on five, ten minutes, all in the middle of a tournament. Meantime, his teammates are sitting on the bench doing their version of Jackie Gleason: "JUST THROW THE BALL!"

Things got so bad he couldn't throw the ball at all. He would not release it from his hand because he couldn't get into the right mind-set. Finally he went to a shrink and they worked it out.

"So what do you do now?" I ask him.

"I just throw the fucking ball! I don't think."

I dug that. And isn't it interesting that after all that, you never once see the Dude bowl in the entire movie. So is thinking the problem? We're so good at it; our brains are set up to think, man.

BERNIE: Thinking's not the problem. We freeze up because we expect a certain result or because we want things to be perfect. We can get so fixated that we can't do anything. Goals are fine; what I don't like is getting caught up in expectations or attachments to a final outcome. So the question is, how do you play freely?

JEFF: Just throw the fucking ball!

Yeah right, only sometimes I care so much. When I was a kid, I stuttered pretty badly. Even now I still stutter every once in a while, feeling like there's something I want to share but I can't get it out. I become anxious and that causes things to get jammed up.

It happens in movies, too. I'll often worry for a long time about a big scene: *How am I going to do this?* Meantime, there's another little scene I'm not concerned about at all, I'm sure I know what to do there. Now comes the day when I'm filming, and the big scene is a snap while the little one is trouble. And I'm reflecting, *All that time you were worried about the wrong thing!* Mark Twain said, "I am a very old man and have suffered a great many misfortunes, most of which never happened."

My brother Beau turned me on to Alan Watts by giving me his book *The Wisdom of Insecurity* when I just started high school. Later I read his other books and listened to his tapes. I've always liked Watts because he wasn't pompous, didn't think of himself as a guru or anything like that, didn't want to convince you of anything, he just liked to share his thoughts with you. And one of them was that if you're going to wait to get all the information you think you need before you act, you'll never act because there's an infinite amount of information out there.

BERNIE: And it's constantly changing. That's why it makes no sense to be attached to outcomes. Only how do you not get attached to outcomes?

JEFF: Just throw that fucking ball. Just do it. Get into the thing, see where it takes you.

I was working with Sidney Lumet on this movie with Jane Fonda called *The Morning After.* His method was to run through the whole movie twice every day. He would tape out the dimensions of all the sets on this gymnasium floor so that we would have a sense of the space we would be acting in. His general direction to us was: "I don't want you to indicate how you're going to do this, I want you to do it. Don't save it. Learn your lines as best you can, get off book, and then just do it."

Sidney was an actor himself; he wasn't afraid of rehearsals. Some actors and directors have this fear that if you rehearse too much, you won't do well when you're actually shooting. You'll do your best work—you'll be your freshest and most spontaneous—in rehearsal, and when the actual filming takes place you'll be stale and just recreate what you did before. I hear their concern. When the camera's rolling, I want it to capture me discovering the character, not re-creating what I discovered or figured out days ago. What I admire and strive for is the kind of acting that shows no apparent obligation to the audience; the audience is just a fly on the wall. In life we're spontaneous, we just orgasm, we just go.

Sidney wanted it fresh, too, but his way of getting this was different. I think he was kind of practicing orgasm, practicing not-practicing. In rehearsals he wanted you to get facile with the role and bring as much to it as you could without holding back. Each time you did that you discovered little things that informed the next time you did it. You had to do it over and over and over again and still come back to emptiness, the place where nothing has been figured out. That's the trap. If you can't get back to emptiness, you're just saying words instead of doing the work, you're just repeating instead of discovering it anew each time.

With Sidney, we practiced starting from scratch. Twice a day we went through the whole movie, so we also learned the story that was being told. Don't forget, when you actually shoot a movie you're shooting out of sequence, so you don't get really steeped in the story even though that's the most important thing. In fact, when you shoot the scenes out of sequence, there's the danger that each particular scene will seem so important that you'll put too much emphasis on it. It's easy to forget that a story is being told.

When we went through the whole movie, we didn't work the scene, we just ran through it once. It was like practicing freshness. He used to say that that was the only way we were going to peel the onion, that each time we did it we were going to discover new things as long as we were fully engaged.

On the day we actually shot the movie, it was a snap. Once we got all the costumes on and were on the set, the scenes just took one or two takes; Sidney would be picking up the batteries, saying, "Let's go, *bubeleh*," and move on to the next setup. We'd all be going at a pretty good clip, and you know what? It felt even fresher than it did during the rehearsals because we were in costume and on the actual location.

When we made *Tucker*, Francis Coppola did a great exercise with Martin Landau and me. The two of us have a strong relationship in the movie, so Coppola said something like this: "I want you guys to do an improvisation right now. We're only going to do it once, but once you do it, you won't have to think about it again because it will be part of your personal history, it will be in your brain. I want you guys to improvise the first day you met. It was on a train and here are the seats." And he pulled out a couple of chairs, putting one next to the other. "Now, Marty, you sit down there. Jeff, you come down and sit next to him. All right, guys—action!"

That improvisation informed the whole movie. You invest, engage in it fully, it becomes a part of you and does its thing.

BERNIE: People get stuck a lot because they're afraid to act; in the worst case, like the master bowler, we get so attached to some end result that we can't function. We need help just to move on, only life doesn't wait.

JEFF: And it doesn't help to say, *I've got to have a mindset with no expectations*, because that's also an expectation. So you can get into a spinning conundrum.

BERNIE: There's a little ditty that sort of sums this up.

JEFF: Hit me with it.

BERNIE: *Row, row, row your boat,*
gently down the stream.
Merrily, merrily, merrily, merrily.
Life is but a dream.

Imagine that you're rowing down a stream and you're trying to figure out how to do it. Do I first row with the right oar and then with the left, or is it the other way around? What does my shoulder do, what does my arm do? It's like Joe, the centipede with a hundred legs, trying to figure out which leg to move first.

JEFF: Art Carney of the centipedes.

BERNIE: He can't get anywhere, just like the person in the rowboat. And while he's hung up with all those questions, the stream is pulling him on and on. So you want to row, row, row your boat—gently. Don't make a whole to-do about it. Don't get down on yourself because you're not an expert rower; don't start reading too many books in order to do it right. Just row, row, row your boat gently down the stream.

JEFF: Merrily, merrily.

BERNIE: That's important. An English philosopher said that whatever is cosmic is also comic. Do the best you can and don't take it so seriously.

JEFF: When I was really young, my mom enrolled me in dance classes. "Mom, I'm too young to dance," I told her. She kind of forced me, but I ended up loving it, and after the first lesson I came back and said, "Come on, Mom, I'll show you the box step." That introduced me not just to dancing but also to working with someone without having a goal; after all, you're not going anywhere, you're just dancing. Years later, whenever she sent me off to work, she'd always say, "Remember, have fun, and don't take it too seriously." So I have this word for much of what I do in life: *plorking*. I'm not playing and I'm not working, I'm plorking.

You know, play doesn't have to be a frivolous thing. You may think of a Beethoven symphony as something serious, but it's still being played. I think Oscar Wilde said that life is too important to be taken seriously.

BERNIE: I always have this red nose in my pocket, and if it looks like I'm taking things too seriously, or the person I'm talking to is taking them too seriously, I put the nose on. It doesn't matter what we're doing or talking about, it doesn't matter if we agree or disagree, the nose changes everything.

JEFF: Clownsville, man. Tightness gets in the way of everything, except tightness.

BERNIE: You can't get arrogant or pompous with a nose. I always tell people that if you get upset over what someone says, imagine him or her with a clown's nose on and you won't get so angry. *Merrily, merrily.* Our work may be important, but we don't take it too seriously. Otherwise, we get attached to one relatively small thing and ignore the rest of life. We're creating a little niche for ourselves instead of working the whole canvas.

Another thing about *Row, row, row your boat gently down the stream.* There are different streams. Sometimes you come to a fall and sometimes you come to white water. Your rowing has to adapt to the situation. You can't do the same stroke coming down a small stream as you would coming down Niagara Falls. Even if you're only rowing down a stream, different things happen: maybe the wind changes, maybe the current, and suddenly everything's different. So *gently* is really important. Don't power yourself or blast through; rock with the way things are. Ask yourself: *What's the deal here? I want to get over there but there are things in the way. How do I flow with the situation? Do I wait or go on? If I wait, do I wait one day, one year, five years? If I go on, do I tack?* Bear witness to the situation and have faith that the right thing to do will naturally arise. Otherwise I get stuck and think, *I can't do anything, everything's all wrong.*

JEFF: And we take it so seriously! Thoughts will change and shift just like the wind and the water when you're on the boat, thoughts are no different than anything else.

Kevin Bacon and I recently worked on a move together, *R.I.P.D.* Just before we'd begin a scene, when all of us would feel the normal anxiety that actors feel before they start to perform, Kevin would look at me and the other actors with a very serious expression on his face and say: "Remember, *everything* depends on this!"

It would make us all laugh. On the one hand, it's not true of course, but on the other, everything *does* depend on this, on just this moment and our attitude toward this moment.

Speaking of boats, there are all kinds. Take a sailboat, for example. Say I want to sail toward you, only the wind is blowing away from you. If I know how to dance with the wind, I can use its power by sailing this way, then that way, and again this way, till finally I get to you. With rowing, you're working primarily with your arms and shoulders. But with sailing, you're making bigger use of the wind and the waves. You're working with more elements, including with your mind and how it perceives things, instead of relying mostly on your own muscles and—

Uh-oh, I'm getting too serious, man. Give me your nose for a second. I need a nose hit. Nostrils go on the bottom, right?

BERNIE: If you want to breathe.

JEFF: I love seeing somebody act real earnest and serious, like Jackie Gleason. He makes me laugh because he reflects back to me my own serious-mindedness and how ridiculous it all is. It's always easier to see somebody else in that position than yourself, and you laugh. It's like the classic slipping on the banana peel, or someone getting hit by a pie in the face. Why do those things make us laugh? Is it from relief, like: *Thank God it wasn't me?* Or is it something else: *I'm being very serious now. I'm pontificating earnestly and solemnly about—* POW! PIE IN THE FACE! The bust-up of certainty. I think that's what makes us laugh, because we all recognize that life's just like that, as uncertain as could be.

BERNIE: When I studied a little clowning, I was assigned a trainer by Wavy Gravy, the famous clown and social activist. My trainer's name is Mr. YooWho and he coordinates the American section of an international group called Clowns Without Borders, which started in Barcelona. They work in war-torn countries all over the world, especially with young kids in refugee camps. I went with him a few times, and what kids all over loved to see was somebody slipping on a banana peel, or else seeing YooWho or me get bopped on the head.

The first time I met YooWho, he had to pick up a computer part at a store in Berkeley, California. The

manager was showing some software to another cus-
tomer and struggling to get a box out from the bottom
of a big pile of boxes. When he finally got it out, the
whole pile of boxes fell right on top of him. YooWho
smiled, shook his head, and said, "You know, I have to
train for weeks to do that."

2.

IT'S DOWN THERE

SOMEWHERE, LET ME TAKE

ANOTHER LOOK

BERNIE: Let me give you a wonderful Zen practice. Wake up in the morning, go to the bathroom, pee, brush your teeth, look in the mirror, and laugh at yourself. Do it every morning to start off the day, as a practice.

JEFF: I've done that on occasion. Give me a definition of practice.

BERNIE: *Row, row, row your boat gently down the stream.* Just like we choose a set of oars to row a boat, we choose oars to awaken; I call those oars practices. And there are all kinds: Zen, Christian, Jewish, Muslim, whatever. Or maybe it's not a spiritual or religious practice but something to do with the arts, or your family, or your work. Maybe it's looking in the mirror and laughing at yourself.

JEFF: For me, it's like clicking into a particular space. You do that in acting because you have to make lots of small adjustments: *Okay, now play the scene this way, now play it that way.* Each time you're making an adjustment you're clicking into a new space.

My father offered me a part in *Sea Hunt* when I was just a kid, and we practiced different basic acting skills. For example, if we were doing a scene together, he'd say, "Don't just wait for my mouth to stop talking before you answer. Listen to what I'm saying and let that inform how you talk back. So if I say things one way, you're going to react one way, and if I say them a different way, you're going to react a different way." Or he'd give me this direction: "Make it seem like it's happening for the first time." And after that: "Now, go out of the room, come back, and do it completely another way. Make a little adjustment."

When you meditate, you also often make small adjustments to get back into the space of simply being.

BERNIE: But most of us aren't just being, we're rowing to get someplace, to some other shore, to a goal or some ideal place we want to reach. So where are we headed? What's the other shore?

In Zen we say that the other shore is right here under our feet. What we're looking for—the meaning of life, happiness, peace—is right here. So the question is no longer, how do I get from here to there? The question is: How do I get from here to here? How do I experience the fact that, instead of having to get *there* for something, it's right here and now? This is it; this is the other shore. In Buddhism we sometimes call it the Pure Land.

In practice, it's hard to grasp that right here, where you're standing, is *it*. You can hear it over and over, but there's a piece of you that doesn't believe it. Instead, we work to get over *there*. And once we get over there, we reconsider: *Oh no, this isn't it, so now I have to get over there.* Off we go again, trying to get to the next other shore. And once we get there, the whole thing starts again. At first I think, *Oh, finally I got somewhere; now I'm happy.* But after a while I say, *No, this isn't it, I've got to get over there.*

JEFF: People often ask me about my other shore, like what other shore do I want to reach. What do I want to be? What do I want to do? Do I want to be a star?

For me, the other shore hasn't really changed. I was kind of thrown into my career at six months old. My father was visiting his friend John Cromwell. At the time, John was directing *The Company She Keeps* and he needed a baby, so my father said, "Here, take Jeff." I never really wanted to be an actor. As a matter of fact, I resisted it because it felt like nepotism to me, that I had the door opened for me by my father. I wanted to be appreciated for my own talents and not because of who my father was. I wanted to do my own thing, and I didn't know what that was because I was interested in so many different things. You can say that I rebelled against the way the river was flowing for me.

At the same time, I would say that the other shore for me was then, and still remains, happiness. And I came to the realization that happiness is right here, available right under my feet. Robert Johnson wrote that the word *happiness* comes from *to happen*. Our happiness is what happens. That's different from the Declaration of Independence, which states that each person has the right to pursue happiness, meaning that if we don't have it we have a right to go after it. But Johnson says that as soon as we pursue it, we lose it. What do you think, Bern?

BERNIE: It's a hard one. Everybody wants to be happy. They want to get to someplace where they're happy, where they're enlightened, where they're content. That's what most people think of when they hear the words *other shore*. They search through books and go to lectures or to gurus, figuring there's got to be somebody to help them get to that other shore, that other space. It's like Dorothy trying to get home in *The Wizard of Oz*. People think of home as the place where they're comfortable and everything's okay. She goes through this whole journey, finds the wizard, and discovers that home is back in Kansas.

JEFF: What does she say in the end? Something about never looking for your heart's desire any further than your own backyard. And the wizard turns out to be a sham, right?

BERNIE: A sham, but also a lure, because the idea that pulled Dorothy all over the Land of Oz is the same idea that pulls us in all directions, too. We think that what we're looking for is somewhere over the rainbow, till we finally realize that it's all just this.

JEFF: We may think that this other shore is something we have to achieve, like fame, success, or enlightenment. But that prevents us from seeing that we're already there. I think the Dude is an example of someone who doesn't feel that he needs to achieve something. He likes lying in the bathtub drinking his White Russians with the whale music on. He's just taking it easy, taking it the way it is. There's a lot of generosity in that, you know? People talk about being seekers, searching for meaning, happiness, whatever. I think of myself as a finder, because I find all these things right around me.

That was also true long ago. When I was a child, my mom had a practice she called Time. She would spend one hour every day with each of her three kids. So if it were my hour, she would say, "What do you want to do today, Jeff?"

And I'd say, "Let's go into your makeup. I'll make you up like a clown and I'll be a monster, let's do that."

"Okay."

Or it might be: "Let's play Space Man. You be the space guy, the spaceship will be under the table, and I'll be the alien trying to get you. And can Tommy come and play with us?"

"Okay, you can invite Tommy."

The phone would ring in the house. "The phone's ringing, Dorothy."

"Tell them I'm having my time with Jeff. I'll call them back."

She was totally focused on me when we had our time, and she did that with each of her kids every day. I never got the feeling that she thought it was her duty; for her it was a gas, she was digging it. Later, when we became teenagers, it would be, "Rub me, Mom," and she'd just massage me for an hour. When I became an adult, I'd give her a call and say, "How about some time, Mom?" Her undivided attention was so nurturing. I never had to seek for anything, like time with my mother, because it was always there.

I also saw how both my parents behaved so generously with other people. I worked with my father in *Sea Hunt* and different movies. As a kid, I sometimes found him a little embarrassing. I remember one occasion when he was doing one of his TV shows and a director was talking to a camera assistant or a PA, getting very angry and not showing respect. My father went up to the director and said in front of everybody, "I will be in my trailer when you're ready to apologize to this guy that you've offended. Come in and let me know." I was so embarrassed! But he had a real sense of honor and justice and would act that way at a drop of a hat.

As an adult, I got to experience the joy he had from his work. He loved all aspects of it and his excitement was contagious. Whenever he came onto a set, people felt, *This guy digs what he's doing. I guess what I'm doing is kind of fun, too.* And everybody got loose and light, which helps things get born. So even if you're dealing with a topic that's not joyful, that's angry, sad, or whatever, if you approach it out of a joyful, generous, loving place, then everything comes out in a freer way. That was the kind of generosity that was available to me when I grew up, and it helped me realize that what makes me really happy is right under my feet.

BERNIE: With all that, I've never met anybody who honestly says all the time, *This is it. This shore, where I'm standing right now, is the place; whatever I need is right here.* Such a person is fully in the moment, here and now, but I've never met anyone who's always like that. No matter how hard we try, situations come up that we'll want to separate from and leave behind us.

But if you *are* going somewhere else, let me say this much: At least change the boat and the oars. Say I get to the other side, what do I do? *Well, I got here thanks to this beautiful boat with the set of oars, so I'll just hold on to them and carry them wherever I go.* Isn't that weird? Now I've got the burden of carrying around whatever got me here. Instead I get rid of it, and I'm free. Time passes and now I want to get to the next other shore. I'll probably need a new kind of boat and different oars, because maybe now the other shore is on the other side of the ocean and that requires a whole other mode of transportation.

When I started my Zen training, enlightenment was the other shore for me. I was sure that if I had an experience of enlightenment, I would understand everything clearly and I would be happy. That first experience did indeed show me that everything is right under my feet and that life as it is, right here this minute, is it; there's no need to look elsewhere. But that realization, big as it was, in some way was still all about me. It could have ended right there—I think it does for some people—but I kept on working and practicing. Finally I realized that practice and enlightenment were endless so enlightenment experiences would keep happening. And since an enlightenment experience is an awakening to the interconnectedness of life, the awakening will keep deepening. It begins with the sense of my self being my body, and it stretches until my self is realized as the universe.

As that understanding grew bigger and deeper, my rowboat changed many times. I still meditate every day, but I've had to learn new practices, too, particularly as I began to work with people who never did meditation.

JEFF: In acting, it's constantly letting go of the rowboat. You do a scene for the first time and you think it was great. Then somebody says, "Oh, no, I'm sorry, there was a hair in the gate, something between the lens and the film, we can't use it." So now you're thinking: *Oh shit, I thought we had that. Now I've got to do it again. Well, gee, it was so good last time, let's see if I can do it exactly like that again.* Instead, you've got to put down the boat, let go of the way you did it before, and get in that empty space again.

Let's say the question is timing. You might think, *See how you paused there two and a half seconds? That was so great, that's the right timing.* That won't be necessarily true the next time around, because everything changes.

BERNIE: To get to a new other shore, we have to choose a different path from the first, like getting a different vessel: rowboat, sailboat, dirigible—

JEFF: —submarine, pogo stick—

BERNIE: —glider. We choose our vessels and the methods to propel them, which are our practices, to get where we want to go. But now there's a problem; something is not right. So maybe we've got to set down the vessel we chose and say, *Okay, here I am. Using that vessel and oars got me into a bad situation, so what should I use instead to get to the next step?* And there's always a next step; it's a continuous practice. Keep on trucking. We say that life flows, but we're always choosing the vessels and the means of propulsion that we want for the next part of the trip. That includes people, too. The people who've had an impact on our lives are also in some way vessels that take us to the other shore. As we aim for a new destination, we often choose new company.

JEFF: Different people have had a strong spiritual impact on me at different times in my life. From the beginning, my mother used to pass around the *Daily Word*, which was my basic spiritual training when I was growing up. It comes from Unity, which is Christian-based and also very open. I think it has a lot of Zen Buddhist leanings. She would pass it around and make all the kids read it.

When I was eighteen, I was in boot camp in the U.S. Coast Guard Reserve for ten weeks. It was the first time I was away from home that long. In boot camp they strip away your identity, they humble and humiliate you, give you a number. One day the company commander says, "All right, assholes, tomorrow is Sunday. All you assholes who wanna go to church fall in this line. All you other assholes fall in this line, you'll have to run on the grinder all day." So of course, everybody goes to church. The priest was a guy named Don Harris, and this is what he told us: "When you're here in this church, you are not in the military. You are in the house of God."

Try to imagine it. Here we are, getting our butts kicked in boot camp, slammed and broken down, and he tells us that we're in the house of God, where our identity and individuality are celebrated rather than crushed. That little reminder meant so much to me. It helped me make an adjustment and click into a whole different consciousness from where I was at the time. Don turned me on to Christianity, though probably not your traditional Christianity. He suggested I read books like Kazantzakis's *The Last Temptation of Christ* and *The Saviors of God*.

He invited me to sing and play my guitar during services. Not the guy to always follow the rules, he gave me some civilian clothes one day when our company was on leave, which you weren't supposed to do, said he wanted to turn me on to something, and took me to the Avalon Ballroom in San Francisco to see Janis Joplin and the Jefferson Airplane. This was long before they had made it.

So Don was very important in my life. In fact, ten years later he married Sue and me.

Two other guys who influenced me were Burgess Meredith and John Lilly. In the early seventies, after making a movie together, Burgess introduced me to John. John Lilly is perhaps most famous for his work with dolphins and interspecies communication, as well as experimenting with LSD. A scientist exploring the nature of consciousness, John invented the isolation tank, a lightless, soundproof tank containing water infused with about a hundred pounds of salt. He was interested in what consciousness is like when the senses have no input from the outside.

He asked Sue and me if we would like to help him out, making us his guinea pigs. Wearing a jumpsuit and looking like some kind of astronaut, John brought me over to the tank and told me to get in, lie down in the water, and get out a total of three times in order to program my mind to know that I could get out if I wanted to. Then I settled back into the buoyant, 98.6-degree water, my ears underwater and my face floating above. I could hear my heart beating and noth-ing else. Almost instantly my mind started kicking in: *John seemed kind of weird—did he have breasts?— what's in this water anyway? PANIC!* Then I caught myself—my mind was just doing its thing—and started to relax.

In some way, I think that was probably the first time I did meditation. I wondered what I could think about, and then realized I could just watch what was happening. I noticed my breathing. I noticed how much mental energy and thoughts I was producing in the tank even when the outside world didn't engage with me at all. In fact, I could almost see my mind as some kind of screen with thoughts and images projected on it. I also began to appreciate the power of my own in-tention to somehow control these projections.

I was in there for three hours. When I came out all the colors and sounds rushed in. I sensed them as never before, appreciating their richness and beauty. I also re-alized that the projections of my mind, so clear to me inside the tank, were continuing to be projected outside the tank. But outside the tank the blankness/emptiness was missing. Instead, my projections were being cast on everything that my senses were receiving, so it was less apparent that so much of the information I had about them was actually coming from inside me. This was a very helpful bit of knowledge and very useful in my life.

I got into Alan Watts and of course, being a child of the sixties, drugs. Watts came from a Christian background like me—in fact, he was a choirboy—before getting into Buddhism, so he could relate to both Christian and Buddhist mythologies. He also dropped acid and got with the culture of the times, like me.

I guess everyone you meet is your guru, teaching you something. But it's like you say, if I want to get to another shore, and another one after that, I change the boat, the oars, and also the people I hang with.

Speaking of boats, I love the term *trim tabbing*, which Buckminster Fuller popularized. You see, giant oceangoing tankers need a giant rudder to make them turn. But engineers discovered that it takes too much energy to turn the giant rudder. Instead, they came up with the trim tab, a tiny rudder attached to the big rudder. The little rudder turns the big rudder and the big rudder turns the ship.

Bucky said that we're all trim tabs. The way to turn society around is to realize that you're connected to something bigger. I like to think that you and I are both trim tabs and that we want to turn other people on to becoming trim tabs and turn the rudder a little bit, which will turn this big ship in the direction where we want to be heading.

3.

DUDE, YOU'RE BEING VERY

UNDUDE

JEFF: The hip counterculture of each generation has sayings that have poetic wisdom for me, words like *dig*, *groovy*, or *grok*. *Karass* is another, from *Cat's Cradle* by Kurt Vonnegut. Your karass is your family in life, not necessarily your biological family. It may even include people you loathe, but they're in your sphere in a very strong way.

Dig is beyond *understand*. I like digging where I am and what I'm doing, I like jamming with myself. So when uptightness happens, I notice that: *You want to be uptight? You can do that; in fact, see how uptight you can get.* Some days I let myself play with it and really go wild. Acting is about tricking yourself, using your imagination to go all over the place. You can do that even if you're not an actor; you can always dance with how you're feeling.

But even playing and jamming require some kind of practice, you know? Preparation is really important to me, especially when I feel tight or afraid.

BERNIE: Practice is critical before you jam with other musicians. But once you start jamming, something happens that you didn't and can't prepare for. Everything starts shifting and you've got a new song coming out, a new riff, and you flow with that because you're jamming. That's what happens in life, too. I can plan and prepare as much as possible, but then I walk down the street and step on a banana peel, and I'm jamming with that.

JEFF: And life will keep throwing it at you, like it does to the Dude. *Oh, you handled this? Well, what about that? And what about that?* It just piles it on.

If you're open, it's not a problem. Take Orson Welles, for example. Have we made many movies better than *Citizen Kane?* What was he, twenty-five years old when he directed that movie? Man! Gregg Toland, the wonderful director of photography, shot that film, and Orson Welles wanted Gregg Toland's name to appear alongside his in the credits at the end because Toland had been so important to the final production of that film. Toland felt the same way toward Welles. He loved that Welles was so new to moviemaking and that his imagination was so open. Welles didn't know anything about making films. I've found the same thing with first-time directors. The jam factor is very high; they don't know what they can't do.

It's also interesting to see how different people react to pressure, including me. You can imagine the pressure on directors. They have a finite time and budget to make a movie, and so much is on their plate every day. *How am I going to do it? I've never done this before.* Problems keep coming up, taking more and more out of them.

With one particular film, right from the beginning of the read-through, I said, "There's something off about that last scene, which is the climax scene for my character." The director and the writers agreed and said we'd fix it together as we got down the line. But the schedule progressed with no time to do that. When you're making a movie, it's like triage, you have to do just what's in front of you, and one problem came up after another. Still, I didn't stop bringing it up to the director.

As we got closer to shooting that scene toward the end of the movie, she would just "show me the hand" when I would come over, sort of like "Shut the fuck up, Donny!" She had a great sense of humor, called me the Prince of Ideas. I got depressed. How was I going to deal with this?

Part of the problem is caring. On the one hand, you want to care, but if your aim is too tight, caring can get in your way. I often write the word *aimless* in my scripts to remind myself not to get my aim so tight that I miss the target. It's a little like what happened to the master bowler, who finally couldn't even release the ball. So I was getting very uptight and she kept putting her hand up every time I came over. We had a few more days before we were going to shoot this scene and I couldn't sleep. I woke up in the middle of the night and said to myself, *Okay now, come on, stop doing this. You're trying to get orange juice out of an apple; figure out what to do.* Then it occurred to me to get help from other people.

I got along well with the director of photography, the producer, and the technical advisor. I went to them and said, "Let me work with you guys and help the director make this the best movie it can be." And that's what they did; they became my virtual director. In the end the scene still wasn't perfect, but it got better. So instead of making it perfect, I made it workable, but not before I was hammered, pressured, and upset; I didn't sleep. And that's just minor stuff. When the big stuff comes, you can get crushed. It's like what the Stranger says in *Lebowski*: "Sometimes you eat the bear, and sometimes, well, he eats you." It gets kind of funky, you know? And what do you do then? You notice: *Oh yeah, this is what I do in these kinds of situations. That's interesting. Do I want to do this now? Is it the best way to get through this? Maybe I should just dig, you know, and jam.*

So perfection is one of the other shores. There are

lots of others: *If I could only be better, if I could only be happier, if I could only be more successful.*

BERNIE: *If I could only be enlightened.*

JEFF: That's a big one.

There was a wonderful Benedictine monk and potter, Brother Thomas Bezanson, who created gorgeous glazes and shapes but was the kind of artist who broke ninety-eight out of every hundred pieces because only two were good enough.

On the other hand, you have an artist like Picasso, who did something similar but in a whole different spirit. He says, *Well, it's like this*, and he draws this scene of the French Riviera.

And you say, *Wow, that's so cool.*

He looks and says, *Nah, but—no, this is not it, maybe—*while you say, *Wait! Wait, you're fucking it up. You're fucking it up. Oh. Oh, I see. Oh, that's interesting. Oh, God, that's beautiful. Okay, just leave it there now. Oh, no, no, you're fucking it up again!*

He does this about five or six times, and then he

crumples up the paper, throws it away, and says, *Now I got some ideas.*

There's nothing precious there. It's all precious, or none of it is, you know what I mean?

BERNIE: There's a whole style of Japanese pottery where the accidents that occur are actually relished by the potters.

When you care about perfection, you care about an expectation. But there is also caring for where I am right now, for what's happening right now. When I spend time with students, they tell me that they've read something in a book or heard something from a teacher that they don't think they're living up to. And I tell them, "Take care of yourself right now. Befriend what's happening, not just who you're supposed to be or what the world should be like. This is where you are now, so how do you care for yourself this minute?"

The only way to do that is to drop the expectation of perfection or any other shore that you have in your head, and jam with what's going on instead. So if part of the situation is that I'm a perfectionist, I'll take care of that perfectionist. I probably know I'm not going to get perfection, there'll always be something a little better, but I'll still care for the guy who wants the perfect sound to come out of that instrument. Not because it's right and not because it's wrong, but because that's who I am this minute and I want to take care of myself.

JEFF: That's got some beauty to it, man.

BERNIE: It gives direction, it gives a path. You've got to take care of yourself on the path, not just when you cross the goal line, because don't forget, wherever you are, that's the goal line.

THE DUDE ABIDES

and

THE DUDE IS NOT IN

4.

YEAH, WELL, YA KNOW,

THAT'S JUST LIKE, UH,

YOUR OPINION, MAN

JEFF: I dig the Dude; he's very authentic. He can be angry and upset, but he's comfortable in his skin. And in his inimitable way, he has grace. He exudes it in every relationship: an unexpected kindness, unmerited good will, giving someone a break when he doesn't deserve it, showing up even when he has a bad attitude just because it means so much to the rest of the team. Hugging it out instead of slugging it out. You know what a *Lebowski* fan told me once? He thought that Donny was a figment of Walter's imagination, an old army buddy of his who may have been killed in Vietnam. And the Dude was going along with the fantasy, participating in the three-way conversation even though he knew Donny didn't exist. I talked to Ethan and Joel Coen about it and they hadn't intended any of that. Either way, it says a lot about the Dude; he can just go with the flow.

BERNIE: You might call him a Lamed-Vavnik. In Jewish mysticism, there are thirty-six righteous people, the Lamed-Vav Tzaddikim. They're simple and unassuming, and they are so good that on account of them God lets the world continue instead of destroying it. But no one knows who they are because their lives are so humble. They can be the pizza delivery boy, the cashier in a Chinese takeout, the window-washer, or the woman selling you stamps in the post office.

JEFF: You also like the word *mensch*, which is German and Yiddish for a real human being. It takes a lot to be a mensch, but the real mensch doesn't know that she's a mensch; she's just living her life.

And what does that mean? My life isn't only my life; everything has brought me to this point: my parents, their parents, everyone before them, and everything else in life, too.

BERNIE: Eons of karma, trillions of years of DNA, the flow of the entire universe—all lead up to this moment. So what do you do? You just do. I think the mensch is not caught up with how to do things or even what to do.

JEFF: And *The Dude abides.* According to Merriam-Webster's official definition, to abide means to wait patiently for something, or to endure without yielding, accept without objection. That is no easy feat, especially in a culture that is success-driven, instant-gratification-oriented, and impatient, like ours. True abiding is a spiritual gift that requires great mastery. The moral of the story, for me, is: be kind. Treat others as you want to be treated. You never know when the stranger you meet on the road may be an angel—or the Dude—in disguise. *I tell you the truth, whatever you did not do for one of the least among you, you did not do for me.*[*] Whether the Dude is a Lamed-Vavnik—

BERNIE: —or Lamed-Lovnik—

JEFF: —an angel in disguise, or merely a kindhearted loser, we should treat him as he treats us, with respect and compassion. We should all treat everyone we encounter as a righteous soul on account of whom the world abides. That's very Dude.

BERNIE: At the same time, the Dude's a lot like us. Stuff upsets him, like when someone pees on his rug. He has thoughts, frustrations, and everything that we all have, but he doesn't work from them. He works from where he is.

---

* Matthew 25:45.

JEFF: He does his thing, he's very authentic, but the chaos of life throws him off time after time. He's rowing his boat merrily, but new things always happen and he has to make an adjustment.

BERNIE: Because there's no perfect place anywhere. One of the Buddha's first teachings was that life is suffering. He didn't just mean heartrending, painful, traumatic suffering, but something more basic than that. It doesn't matter how good we have it or how basically happy we are, things arise every day that leave us feeling discontented or disappointed.

So the movie opens up with a bit of suffering for the Dude because somebody peed on his rug, the rug that ties the room together. Till now he was just rowing his boat merrily down the stream, taking his baths, drinking his White Russians, listening to whales, and bowling. But now something happened, so he makes an adjustment, goes out to meet the wealthy Mr. Lebowski, and the movie goes on from there. At exactly the point when the rug doesn't bother him anymore, something else comes up. And when he's no longer upset about that, there's something else. Things keep happening and the suffering gets deeper. Why? Because the Dude expects that nothing else is going to go wrong. He's like everyone else, thinking that around the corner is some perfect place where everything will be okay; all he has to do is round that corner. Then something else comes up, and something else.

But the Dude abides, so it doesn't take him too long to be at ease with the new situation. Not so his bowling buddy Walter. Walter plays the Dude's great foil: *This won't stand, man.* He's like all the rest of us. Someone just found out that he has cancer, or that his wife left him for someone else, or that he lost his job. Unexpected things keep happening, which is what the Buddha referred to when he talked of suffering. And what do we say? *This won't stand, man.* But that's what life is, constant change, ups and downs. And like the Dude, we have to abide. Walter, on the other hand, can't accept that life is this way, so he keeps on suffering.

JEFF: I love the scene when the Dude is freaking out at Walter: "Will you just take it easy?"

And Walter says, "Calmer than you."

"Walter, take—will you take it—"

"Calmer than you."

People think the Dude is so unflappable and calm, but in that scene he's really uptight. In fact, the whole movie is about this loose, relaxed guy who gets all upset by life. But he's not embarrassed about it, he's not trying to live up to some persona, he's always the Dude.

I relate to that because I really dig comfort. And part of being comfortable is living up to others' expectations of you. For instance, many people think I have this persona, that I'm the Dude. But that's not who I am. I got some Dude in me, but I'm more and other than that. I can get tight and nervous, and unlike the Dude, I'm not always comfortable showing people those cracks in my persona.

I'll give you an example. Thomas Nellen has done my hair and makeup for several movies. He's a wonderful Swiss guy, very meticulous, a great artist, and we like to talk and share ideas when I'm getting made up. One of his jobs is to provide continuity and consistency in how I look for the movie. For example, my hair always has to look right for each scene, so if it's cut a certain way for my character and the character ages, the hair also has to age. If the character doesn't age in the movie, the hair has to look the same even if the filming

65

takes months. And don't forget, you're shooting out of sequence all the time, so the hair has to be right for whatever scene you're filming that day. It's Thomas's job to pay attention to all these little details. Making movies is all about the tiny details. It's like doing a magic trick. When you create an illusion, the audience doesn't want to see how it's done. If a guy has a fake nose, you don't want to see the lines between the real thing and the fake, you want it all to look real, and for that there has to be consistency. If it's a little off, the audience loses the spell and gets out of the story.

So at the end of an especially stressful day Thomas wants to cut my hair a little. That's his job, right? And he's very respectful. "When do you want to have your hair cut, Jeff? It's getting longer and longer."

But I have this thing going on with my hair that dates back to the time when I was a kid, when having my hair cut and getting the clippings in my shirt drove me crazy. I could never get the hair out. It also feels a little like Samson: you cut your hair and you lose your power. Or it's like the superstitions in sports, when somebody says, "Hey, don't you want to wash those socks?"

And you say, "No, these are my lucky socks, don't touch them."

"Awww, come on, wash your socks. What's the difference?"

"Don't touch my socks, man!"

All these things are going on, I'm feeling irritable and I want to get home, so I keep putting him off: "If you cut my hair now you'll have to cut it again later, and I want my hair to be as long as I can have it for the next movie." Thomas would also be working on that one.

And he says, "Yes, Jeff, but you've now gone three weeks without a cut."

And I say, "Thomas, my hair has to be long for the part anyway. If I was supposed to be bald and hadn't shaved my head in three weeks, you'd notice. But with this much hair, nobody's going to see any difference."

The argument goes on, and finally I give up: "Okay, just cut my fucking hair. You're the makeup guy, you're the expert, go on, do it."

So he's cutting my hair while I sit there trying to meditate, right? I do an angry meditation for a half-hour, all that time feeling and hearing every little snip. Finally he's done and I say, "Thank you, I appreciate your conscientiousness." But I am pissed.

So now I go home and I've got two days off. For those next two days I can't sleep because this hair thing keeps coming up. I'm thinking, *What are you doing? Why are you obsessing about this? It's ridiculous.* But I'm just churning it over and thinking about it all day and all night. At the same time I'm reading about the Tibetan Lojong practices, which are basically slogans all about leaning into these uncomfortable situations and opening up to them as if they're gifts. One in particular strikes me: *Always maintain a joyful mind.* Appreciate the struggles as opportunities to wake up.

After two days I get back to work: "Thomas, how you doing, man?"

He goes, "I'm fine."

I say, "Well, I was fucked. For the last three nights I haven't slept at all, I keep on thinking about this ridiculous hair thing."

And Thomas says, "To tell you the truth, I felt shitty the whole weekend, too."

And finally the whole thing shifted. It started looking like a segment from *30 Rock* or *The Office*, you know? We laughed about it and I told him what I'd gone through. I mean, we're talking about a quarter inch of hair and look at all the stuff that came up! That's what I mean by wanting to live up to expectations. I'm supposed to be so cool, and look at how upset I'm getting about almost nothing.

I said, "This has a lot of juice for us, man. This can be our hair koan."

Thomas said, "What do you mean?"

So I suggested we do something that my wife and I do sometimes. We sit opposite each other. One person expresses what's on his or her mind and the other person just listens and receives, till the first person has no more to say, and then we switch. We keep on doing that till both of us feel like we're done. Sometimes the shift happens, sometimes it doesn't; it's a jam. So Thomas and I did this and we found a lot of humor and intimacy in it. It was uncomfortable for both of us, but it also deepened our relationship because all these little bumps and discomforts are actually opportunities to explore and keep the curiosity going: *Oh, this is interesting, what's this about? Why did I get so upset?* That's what I mean by leaning into things. And here was an opportunity for Thomas to see this: *Hey, you think I'm a calm, cool, easygoing guy. Truth is, I can be tight and pissed and as dumb as the next guy.* There's embarrassment there, you know? It's like the Dude freaking out and Walter keeps saying, "Calmer than you. Calmer than you."

People think I'm laid-back and that nothing gets to me, and it's embarrassing to show them a whole other side. But if I acknowledge it rather than deny it, it also can be the path to healing instead of obsessing about it at home: *That goddamn Thomas has no idea. Doesn't he understand that it's not about simply matching the hair, that there's an inner life to the actor that he shouldn't interfere with?* You can pump it up and defend yourself all you want, but you're just suppressing the self-consciousness and the embarrassment, you know? With Thomas I worked it out by just being who I am without living up to something.

But the Dude isn't uncomfortable with his discomfort. He's authentic, and he and Walter jam with each other. He can get pissed at Walter but he loves him at the same time. I love that scene where they hug in the end, with Donny's ashes all over the Dude, coating his shades.

BERNIE: The other thing I like about the Dude is that he doesn't corner a rat. Do you know that expression? If people do things we don't like, we sometimes set them up in order to show them how wrong or bad they are. It's like trapping a rat. If you force a rat into a corner where there's no way out, it's going to attack. You don't see the Dude doing that. He's opinionated, but he leaves the other person a way out. Walter constantly tries to trap the rat, pushing people into a place where they're now going to fight back.

JEFF: You have to leave a way out. In Zen, don't they tell you to kill yourself? I don't mean literally, but to kill your ego, kill your identity. Isn't that the way out in Zen?

BERNIE: A lot of old Zen masters talked like that. They said that in order to get enlightened, in order to experience the oneness of life, you had to drop body and mind. But there's an easier way out than that, and that's to realize, *Oh, that's just your opinion*, which is what the Dude says in the movie: "That's your opinion, man." When you say that, there's always a way out. If we take certain things to be *the* truth, we're going to fight and kill for them, but it's hard to battle over an opinion.

JEFF: You can respect opinions. You both have the same thing going on, only you have your version of it and someone else has theirs.

BERNIE: One of the most famous figures in Zen in China is known as the Sixth Patriarch, Huineng. He was an illiterate peasant who cut wood to support his mother and himself. One day he goes to the market to sell his wood and hears a monk chanting a line from the *Diamond Sutra*: "Abiding nowhere, raise the Mind." If you can abide nowhere, you are raising the mind of compassion. So here's this guy who knows nothing about Buddhism, a woodcutter, but when he hears that verse he has a profound enlightenment experience.

JEFF: Did he know what the words meant?

BERNIE: No. Enlightenment doesn't happen because you understand some words. You could say that the words triggered his transformation, but actually it was his whole life that brought him to that place of hearing a verse and experiencing a deep enlightenment.

So he asked the monk where he heard this, and the monk said that there's a monastery up north where they teach this kind of stuff. He goes north and the abbot says, "Why are you here? You're a southerner." In that period, the northern Chinese considered the southern Chinese inferior. According to the story, Huineng answered: "In the Way there is no difference between north and south." The true nature of the Way, of life, is that it's all one, there are no differences.

It turns out that the abbot was getting ready to retire and was looking for a successor. It was a big monastery, with some monks who'd been training for twenty, thirty years; naturally, everybody thought one of them would take over. But the abbot recognized Huineng as his successor just from this answer. Still, instead of accepting him into the monastery, the abbot sent him to work in the rice mill.

One night he went to the rice mill and told Huineng that he's making him his successor, the next in the lineage of Zen masters. But he warned him that the others would kill him, because they'd been training for so long and believed it should be one of them, not some illiterate woodcutter from the south, so he advised him to run for his life. He gave Huineng the robe and the bowl, which are signs of transmission, and Huineng escaped.

Sure enough, one of the head monks, a former general, chased him down. When Huineng saw that the monk was catching up with him, he left the robe and bowl on the ground and hid behind a rock. The monk tried to pick them up, but he couldn't lift them. Full of fear, he apologized to Huineng and asked him for a teaching. Huineng asked him: "What was your original face before your parents were born?" That's like asking, what is there before your parents and their parents, before anything and anyone you can conceive of? At that point, the monk had an enlightenment experience. He thanked Huineng, but Huineng told him not to forget his many years of practice and training under the old abbot. He's your teacher, Huineng said, this is just a moment, like the crest of a wave that has traveled the seas for a long time.

Certain moments can set something off, but it won't happen without lifetimes of work beforehand.

Abiding nowhere, raise the mind of compassion. The Dude abides nowhere, which is the same as saying that the Dude abides everywhere. The Dude is not attached to some self-image, identity, or a life narrative. Since he abides nowhere, he is free to abide everywhere.

JEFF: As he says in his phone message, *The Dude is not in.*

BERNIE: If you abide in one particular place, you're stuck, because you're attached. On the other hand, if you abide everywhere, in the whole world, you're not attached to anything, so you're free. As soon as you get attached—*Hey, he peed on my rug!*—you're abiding somewhere and the suffering begins.

JEFF: Shunryu Suzuki, who founded the San Francisco Zen Center, said that if something is not paradoxical, it's not true. If you say that abiding nowhere is the same as abiding everywhere, then abiding and not abiding are kind of the same thing, too. It can get very confusing, and true at the same time.

BERNIE: I believe that's because we're steeped in Aristotelian logic, where you can't abide and not abide at the same time. But light is both a wave and a particle. When you're stuck to it just being one or the other, you don't see the whole thing. So we need a new kind of paradigm, one that will help us perceive that you can be here and not be here at the same time.

JEFF: Heraclitus, a Greek philosopher who preceded Aristotle, was the guy who said that you could never step in the same river twice, because the river's always changing. And I'm always changing, too; I'm not the person I was a minute ago. So one does not equal one, because there are no two ones that are exactly the same.

BERNIE: And that's your opinion, man.

JEFF: That's right, that's my opinion. *Two . . . two . . . two mints in one!*

5.

PHONE'S RINGIN', DUDE

JEFF: We got shook out in L.A. with the earthquake in 1994. That earthquake was something; have you ever been in one?

BERNIE: There was a big one in Los Angeles way back, around 1970, and the Valley really got hit. I was sitting in the meditation hall. The building shook pretty hard but we sat through the whole thing.

JEFF: We were living on the edge of Santa Monica Canyon, on a street called Adelaide. Later I saw a small map of the faults and realized that we had our own little fault right around our house. I usually sleep naked, and that night—BOOM! I thought it was war or an invasion from outer space. Glass was breaking all over the place. I got up and raced to the other end of the house to get the kids, trying not to step on the glass. And then there were the aftershocks. I'd lived in L.A. all my life, but I'd never experienced an earthquake like that one. It would stop and then go on, again and again.

I still remember the problem of turning off the gas in the house. You want to do that right away in such a situation, and I always think of that as a man's thing, you know, going down to the basement in the middle of an earthquake while upstairs your wife and kids are standing under the doorway. But I was away so much making movies that I had no idea where the gas valve was, so instead it was my wife, Sue, who went down to turn it off while I huddled upstairs with my daughters under the doorway.

We spent the rest of the night in the front yard in sleeping bags, wondering what was going to happen. But when we woke up, life was back to normal, guys pedaling on their bikes, everybody acting almost as if nothing had happened, in complete denial.

But it had a big impact on me. We rely so much on the ground being stable and it's a shock when it starts moving and shaking instead. That night left me with a profound feeling of fear and the realization that there was absolutely nothing to count on. Before the earth-quake I counted on the earth staying in one place; I didn't think about it, I just took it for granted. But after-ward I realized that anything can happen. I also became aware of the possible function of denial in allowing us to carry on in some sort of fashion, helping us forget how precarious and transitory the universe really is.

People had made an adjustment.

BERNIE: In life we have to make adjustments because everything is always changing. You know what this re-minds me of? Hens lay eggs to have little chicks. When the chick is ready to come out of the egg, it pecks at the eggshell: *peck peck peck peck peck*. Hearing that, and sensing it's the right time, the hen clucks a little bit and also goes *peck peck peck peck peck*, using her beak to peck from the outside. Together, they break the shell and the chick is born. If the hen does it too soon, the chick dies, because it's not fully formed. If the hen does it too late, the chick suffocates. So timing is really important here.

In the same way, in every instant there's a new universe or a new me about to be born. If you're attuned enough, you can hear the pecking of the universe saying, *Peck peck peck peck peck, I want to be born!* Maybe it's a new Jeff that wants to be born, or a new Bernie, or a whole new world. I'm outside and I want to help, so I have to peck back. But what tool do I use to give birth to this new world? I'm not a hen. I've got choices. I've got a screwdriver, I've got love, I've got an elbow, I've got lots of different tools.

We have a figure in Zen, sort of a fat guy, looks a little bit like Santa Claus without a beard.

JEFF: I know him; it's Hotei, right? Sue gave me a beautiful wood sculpture of Hotei to put in my office.

BERNIE: Hotei's got this bag full of tools and those tools are everything in the world. He's got talcum powder, he's got condoms, he's got a screwdriver.

JEFF: Vibrator in there, you think?

BERNIE: He's got a vibrator, he's got books, whatever you can think of. That bag contains every object that exists, and he walks around the marketplace talking to everybody he meets and taking care of them using those tools.

You know who that reminds me of? You live in Santa Barbara. I used to live there, and whenever I saw Jonathan Winters walking around Montecito he always reminded me of Hotei.

JEFF: Did you hang with him at all? I first met him with my parents when I was a kid. Some thirty years later I ran into him in Santa Barbara shopping in a pharmacy aisle. I felt from him an immediate familiarity. He went straight into character with the raspy Maude Frickert voice, and I assumed some bizarre voice. We just kept going and going. Finally we both broke out of it and started talking about painting. He paints, too, you know.

BERNIE: Hotei is a little like that. He walks places and hears the pecking—*peck peck peck peck*—of what needs to be born, and he reaches into the bag and pulls out the right tool to allow the birth to happen. In Zen, our ideal of training is that we become simple, like Hotei, like a mensch. Nothing special, just Jonathan Winters walking around Montecito talking to anybody. We listen to the pecking of the universe wanting to be born and take out an appropriate tool to help that happen.

So Hotei, who can be a man or a woman, is a great Bodhisattva,[*] a great mensch. To the extent that he abides nowhere, which means that he abides everywhere, he can help more people.

JEFF: Let me tell you what popped into my mind: I'm having a great outing with my buddy Dawa, a Tibetan Buddhist. We're walking in the hills of Santa Barbara to an old hotel that burned down about a hundred years ago. We're feeling like Indiana Jones exploring the old stone foundations. There are also these great hot springs up there. We go in and the mineral water bubbling out of the ground is just the perfect temperature, not one degree too hot or too cold. We soak in all those great minerals, feeling great, and then we start going back,

---

* In Zen Buddhism, a person who, motivated by compassion, vows to work for the complete enlightenment of all beings.

talking dharma stuff together and getting off on it. We notice that as we walk side by side, one of us may stumble or even slip and the other catches him reflexively, just like you catch yourself when you're going off balance. And I'm thinking, *Oh yeah, this is interconnectedness, man, self as other, this is oneness, this is nirvana*, you know, walking down the hill like we're one and feeling great.

All of a sudden, a crazy man comes down the trail—I mean, quivering crazy. And he's pissed, frightening, like a demon or something. And all my airy-fairy stuff goes WHOMP! Instead I start thinking, *I hope he doesn't hurt me. I'm glad I've got my dogs, I'm glad I've got this Tibetan guy, maybe he knows some kind of jujitsu to defend us.* There's nothing in my heart like *What can I do to help you, man? You look a little troubled.* He passes us and then he looks back and says, "You want to fuck with me?" And I'm not so high anymore and full of all those ideas.

Life does that to you constantly, like the earthquake. You think you've got it together? WHOMP! And what we try to do is get one up on life, figure it out, get enlightened, whatever, just so it won't trip us up again.

BERNIE: We all have different degrees of realization, of seeing the oneness of life, and our job is to actualize this understanding. It's a lifelong, endless path. But you know what your story reminds me of? Those dolls that are full of sand at the bottom. You push them and they oscillate quickly from side to side, and then come back to center. So as you practice, you're filling up with sand. At first, even a weak force hits you and almost knocks you over, but you oscillate in big arcs till you come up standing again. As you practice more and more, it takes a stronger and stronger force to get you knocked over, and even then the oscillations aren't so big, and before you know it you're back to center.

JEFF: It's not like you *never* get knocked over.

BERNIE: No matter how much sand you put in, no matter how much you practice, there will always be some force that's big enough to knock you over. Life's not about not getting knocked over, it's about how fast you come back. So if you think, *Oh, I got knocked over and that's a sign that I'm not practicing well enough*, all that happened was that you met a situation that was a little bigger than you, and that gave you a new opportunity for more practice.

JEFF: Situations like that sometimes cause me to shy away from taking chances and doing things, because I feel that nothing I do is ever going to be enough. Or maybe it's always enough.

BERNIE: What matters is that you do it; everything else is extra.

JEFF: Speaking of the hen and the chicken, the hen doesn't just have one egg, she's got a bunch, so which does she tend to? What do I tend to? Do I tend to the pain in myself, to someone who wants help, or to that piece of wood over there that I'd like to carve something out of?

BERNIE: It's like your body. Your wrist and finger get cut. Which one are you going to tend to first? Naturally, you deal with the wrist first.

JEFF: Tending to the wound that needs it the most. Life as triage.

BERNIE: There's only a problem if you get frustrated. *Oh, there's too much going on, I can't take care of everything. I cut my wrist and I cut my finger, it's too much to handle!* People can get so frustrated they don't do anything.

JEFF: Being alive, you have to do something. Not doing anything is also some kind of action.

BERNIE: When he was very young, my son, Marc, would look at his plate, and if it had foods on it that he didn't like he would say, "Gross choices." But even with gross choices, you have to do something. All the second-guessing and thinking—*Should I have done more? Should I have done less?*—are extra. You open up to the degree that you do; all the rest is internal commentary, which is not necessary. It's already done, man.

JEFF: Like Popeye's *I am what I am*, right? *And that's all that I am*.

BERNIE: *I am that I am.* That was God's answer to Moses when Moses asked Him for His name.* My wife, Eve, likes to say: *That's that.*

JEFF: Going back to the chicken pecking, you have to be sensitive to hear the pecking. But you can have too much sensitivity and then you often need earplugs, you know? We say that we want to be more alive and sensitive to hear the pecking and respond in a timely way, but sometimes life can get too loud: *Please, there's a racket, I need some earplugs*, or *It's too bright, I need some dark glasses here.* To use the analogy of the hen and the egg, maybe the hen has really fine hearing. She thinks she hears the chick pecking so she pecks back at the egg, only it's too early and the chick dies. Or else she's covered up her overly sensitive ears and now can't hear too well.

* Exodus 3:14.

BERNIE: Meantime, the little chick inside, or whatever needs to be born, is screaming, *Let me outta here! Let me outta here!* In some sense, once the screaming starts it's already too late. So you befriend yourself and say, *Okay, next time I'll respond earlier, I'll listen better.* In my opinion, the screaming is a sign not that you were too sensitive but that you waited too long. Timing's critical. If we wait too long, the chick suffocates.

JEFF: Sometimes it feels so intense that I need to dull myself, or just try to relax, like I do with cigars. You also like cigars. How do cigars jibe with, you know, the view that the body is the temple and all that stuff?

BERNIE: The body *is* the temple, so you should offer it some incense. There are a number of traditions where tobacco is used almost as a sacrament, like with the Sufis and the Native Americans. But I don't want to put it on such a high plane, I just dig cigars.

JEFF: It's a kind of refuge, man. Buddhism has three refuges, right?

BERNIE: Buddha, Dharma, and Sangha. The awakened one, his teachings, and the community of practitioners who vow to awaken as he did.

JEFF: There are also false refuges, refuges you think will ease the pain but in the long term cause even more, like booze or drugs. Some people will say cigars, too. I'm kind of a slow learner, or I learn at my own speed, and I've done many different things to take the edge off, so to speak, to distract me and help me relax. Otherwise that sensitivity is too intense.

BERNIE: Knowing when is the appropriate time to act is a learning curve. That's true in acting also, right? If you don't respond at the right time the director yells at you, "It's too late!" Or if you respond too quickly: "It's too soon! Why are you rushing in here?"

Luckily, we have practices to build up our sensitivity and improve our sense of timing. One practice is: *The Dude is not in.* When you're not attached to Jeff and I'm not attached to Bernie, when we see we're not separate from each other and the rest of the world, we can now raise the mind of compassion, no longer working just on our own behalf but for the sake of all beings. It's no longer about me; it's about everything and everyone in the universe. My first awakening experience was great, and it caused me to be a tough Zen guy demanding that everyone else in the meditation hall practice hard to have the same experience. But the second one was much broader. It wasn't about me or other practitioners; it was about all the hungry spirits in the world. And that's everyone, including you and me.

In Zen Peacemakers we have Three Tenets, and the first is *not knowing*, which corresponds to abiding nowhere, being in that state of non-attachment. That's *The Dude is not in*. If I say, *Bernie's not in*, in most cases there is still some Bernie left in, some attachment I have to an aspect of myself. It could be as basic as my attachment to being a man, a teacher, or a father. Those may all be very positive things, but if I'm attached to them then they'll condition me, and they will limit the possibilities of action in my life.

Say I identify too much with the teacher part of me. If someone asks me for help, I may give her a lecture about Zen when what she really needs is some listening, money, or just a big hug. My conditioning to teach will limit my flexibility and responsiveness.

It's very rare to be in a state where there's nothing in, where you have no attachment to any idea or concept about yourself. In that state you've immediately raised the mind of compassion, because if nothing is in, everything is in, and you are now free to experience yourself as the world. Much of Zen training is about helping us get to that state.

The second of the Zen Peacemakers Tenets is bearing witness to the joys and suffering of the world, which means not backing away from anything that comes up inside you or that you see and hear in life.

JEFF: There's a difference between somebody who is enlightened and someone who thinks, *It's all me, it's all for me.* That's seeing things only from your conditioning, only from your opinions, which is the opposite of not being in.

One of the cool things about acting is that it's all about getting inside other people's skin, other people's reality. I've played some sociopaths and psychopaths. Of course, the sociopath doesn't view himself as a sociopath; it's all a matter of perspective. So what is the correct perspective? Wherever you're standing, you're going to see something else, right?

Take the characters in *Jagged Edge* or *The Vanishing*. *The Vanishing* is about a guy who buries people alive. *Jagged Edge* is about a sociopath who kills his wife. What I discovered in my exploration of those characters, especially with the guy in *The Vanishing*, is that he's alive. He senses his aliveness; he feels the world and the people in it as extensions of himself. In a way, he wants to express himself and even serve people, only his way of doing that is burying them alive. So we all have different views of what it is to serve others. It goes back to *That's your opinion, man.*

The character in *The Vanishing* is a little like Jack Nicholson when he says, in *A Few Good Men*, "You can't handle the truth." *You can't handle that you need some motherfucker like me who's willing to do your dirty work.* So the character in *The Vanishing* says, *I'm gonna murder these people, and it's a blessing because it's good for the whole.* Hitler might have felt the same way, and all those others who do terrible things. They had their dream and their vision; they were capable of love and all the basic human emotions. So why do we call one dream good and another one bad?

BERNIE: For me it's about not-knowing and bearing witness. *The Dude is not in* refers to a pure state of no attachment whatever, nothing there. That's not true about the characters you described. As you said, the guy in *The Vanishing* thinks of people as extensions of himself, which is the opposite of *The Dude is not in*. When we bear witness to something, there's almost no distance between myself and what I'm observing, between subject and object. In acting, you get completely inside the skin of the character you're playing; you totally bear witness to him or her. I call the actions you do out of that, *loving actions*. If the characters you played were bearing witness to the people they killed, their loving actions would have been pretty different from what they ended up doing. Imagine bearing witness to what it feels like to be buried alive! There's no way he'd do what he did.

Taking loving actions is the Third Tenet of the Zen Peacemakers. In terms of practice, we have to learn how to bear witness to all these folks, including the sociopaths and the psychopaths, and then the appropriate loving action arises.

JEFF: Because all those folks are us. We're all aspects of the same thing.

BERNIE: Part of my practice is to try to bear witness to everything that feels ugly or that scares me. That's why I started to do our yearly retreats at the Auschwitz-Birkenau concentration camps in Poland, where 1.3 million people were murdered. I meet all aspects of myself there: victims, killers, children, guards, bureaucrats, even the electrified fences that surrounded the place. All of them are nothing but me.

My definition of enlightenment is realizing the oneness of life. And whatever you exclude and call *not me*, or whatever you're not willing to deal with, is going to thwart you. Any action you take that does not include all viewpoints is going to fail, and it will fail exactly in the areas you excluded.

Lenny Bruce liked to say, *What's the deal here?* In each of these situations, what's the deal here? What are we leaving out? Who are we leaving out? That's where we're going to have problems. We're everything and everyone, and that's whom we should bring to the table. Instead, we invite the people we feel good about and we leave out the others. But those people are still us. We're going to fall short wherever and whenever we put on blinders and refuse to deal with everyone.

So bearing witness to as many people as possible is very important. But in order to do that we have to be totally not in, with no attachments whatsoever, and as I said before, I've never met the person who's completely not in. We are in to a certain degree and we're not in to a certain degree. We have attachments to some things and not to others. The world pecks away, sending us messages; we listen to some, and we don't listen to others. We bear witness to some; we don't bear witness to others. One message may be this nightmarish guy that's burying people alive, like your character in *The Vanishing*, only we don't want to bear witness to him, he's too scary. Another may be Adolf Hitler. We don't want to bear witness to him, either, we want him dead. But if we do bear witness to the part of humanity that all these different people represent, we grow, and our loving actions will reflect that, too.

JEFF: There's also an aspect of how quickly and deeply we're ready to go. There's a story of the Hindu god, Brahma. One of his angels comes to the king and says, "Brahma would like to show himself to you. How would you like him to show himself? Think about it and give me your answer."

Then he goes to a very humble man, not a king by any means, and says the same thing: "Brahma's going to show himself to you. Think about how you would like him to show himself."

The next day the angel goes back to the king, who says: "I would like Brahma to show himself to me and all of my subjects in his full glory. And since I've got some meetings at noon, I'd like that to happen at, say, eleven o'clock."

The angel agrees. Eleven o'clock rolls around, the king's guys assemble, Brahma shows himself in all his glory, and they all disintegrate because they can't handle his full glory. There's nothing left, not even ashes; they're just gone.

Then the angel goes to the humble man and asks, "How do you want Brahma to show himself?"

The man answers, "I want Brahma to show himself in all of the faces that I see every day, in ordinary life." That's what he gets, and he doesn't die because he took the glory in manageable doses.

So the question is, how much are you ready to take on? How much are you ready to bear witness to? What's it going to cost you?

6.

NEW SH** HAS COME TO LIGHT

JEFF: T Bone Burnett told me this about performing with my band: You don't have to feel like you're pulling the train. When you're up there on the stage with the rest of the band, you're opening the door for them to go through. You don't have to push them—*Come on, we gotta do this!*—thinking that otherwise it's not going to get done. It's more of a moving out of the way than trying to muscle it through.

BERNIE: When you first start doing Zen meditation, we give this instruction: *Thoughts will come; the brain's job is to produce thoughts. Don't try to stop them, and also don't follow them. Pretend it's an open door; let the thoughts come in and let them go. Don't try to manipulate them because you'll get into trouble.*

I love talking about Zen and jazz bands. We're instruments of life. You perfect your instrument, which is yourself, to become a player. But playing in a band, where you hear the sounds of all the instruments, is very different from playing alone.

JEFF: Playing in a band makes you bigger. It takes you to places you'd never go just on your own.

BERNIE: Imagine if you're sitting there as part of the band and you say, *I'm gonna play these chords no matter what the other guys do.* It kills the whole thing.

JEFF: Or *I'm gonna force these guys to do what I do.* You don't get the benefit of hearing another aspect of yourself. The creativity's gone.

It's a little like that when I work on a movie. I can see that everyone is different, that we serve different purposes and are all aspects of the whole. For instance, one of the things that I find very freeing in making a movie is to turn it over to the director. I hold his opinion above mine unless I get something that comes from a higher power; if it's that intense, I'll be subversive and try to sneak my way in there. But generally, I like to empower the director and give him power over me so that I can transcend myself and make something bigger than what I have in my own mind, maybe even surprise myself. All the folks there have different opinions and visions of what's going on, which enrich my experience and also make for a better movie.

My stand-in, Loyd Catlett, is a deep friend. He's from Texas, a hunter with trophies on his wall, and was raised very differently from me. I've probably spent almost as much time with him as I've spent with my wife. My father's name was spelled with two *l*s, Catlett's name is spelled with one. Over the last forty-five years we've done around sixty films together. That may be a record: *Most Movies Made by an Actor & Stand-in Team*. I met him on *The Last Picture Show* in 1971 and he's been the thread that runs through most of my movies.

The stand-in's job is to work with the director of photography to set up the lights and cameras before the actual shooting takes place. This can be tedious and go on for hours, but Loyd is a professional and he knows how I move and speak, which is very helpful in getting the movie made.

We have a wonderful relationship; he's invaluable to me in so many ways, not only as a stand-in and occasional stuntman but also as my role model for many roles, from *The Last Picture Show* to *True Grit*. Anytime I'm playing a western character, he's my go-to guy. And beside all that, he's my dear friend. Being a Texan, he's got a lot of one-liners that are music for the soul, like, "You know what your problem is? You don't realize who I think I am." Or sometimes he switches it: "You know what my problem is? I don't realize who you think you are."

We have different skill sets and different opinions about things, but all are useful perspectives and tools.

BERNIE: So how do I just let it all be, bear witness, and get into the swing? I love Ellington's tune, "It Don't Mean a Thing (If It Ain't Got That Swing)." Just let it be. Bear witness to the voices and the instruments—whether it's a jazz band or life—and then move with them, flow with them. If you can do that, then you'll be a lot happier because in life you're always in a band and you're always swinging. You're not forcing anything and you're not being forced, you just flow. Like your friend T Bone said, people think that if you're not figuring it out and forcing it in certain ways, you're not going to get things done. The opposite is true. You'll get more done because you're allowing the creativity to flow.

To paraphrase Linji, founder of the Rinzai school of Zen, the whole world is a puppet stage, so who's pulling the strings?* If you're in there pulling the strings and telling people what they have to do, it's not going to be a great puppet show.

JEFF: Or, going back to *The Dude is not in*, if you really are not in, and that's what's pulling the strings, that's pretty fucking cool.

---

* Linji Yixuan said, "Behold the puppets prancing on the stage, and see the man behind who pulls the strings."

BERNIE: As soon as you know something, you're not completely open and you can't bear witness to life. Bearing witness is like plunging, becoming completely one with something. Meditation is a practice for not-knowing and bearing witness. When you just sit, you let go of thoughts and feelings and bear witness to what arises moment after moment.

In Zen we have different practices to help us do that. There are koans, like what Huineng said to the monk who pursued him: *What was your original face before your parents were born?* Your brain tells you that it makes no sense. You let go of that, you go into the state of not-knowing, bear witness to the koan, and something happens.

I've developed the practice of doing street retreats, where a small group of us lives on the streets without ID or money and just with the clothes on our backs. That's a plunge into life on the streets. Things become gritty and immediate; instead of worrying about business or work, you're thinking about where to get your next meal, how far away it is, where you can use a bathroom, and where you can sleep. For a short while, you become one with the streets. No matter what your life is like back home, during that week you feel raw and vulnerable. Another plunge is our annual retreats at the Auschwitz-Birkenau concentration camps. You can read books and see movies about Auschwitz all you want, but it has nothing to do with the experience of being there.

If we go back in history, Zen masters used shouting and hitting to get you to the place where you're not in, where you abide nowhere. When we have some sense of self, we feel secure. But when there's a shout or a hit—

JEFF: —it clears everything. That sense of self is gone.

BERNIE: That's what I look for when I work with students. I'm not interested in their understanding terminology or reciting scriptures, I want them to embody *The Dude is not in*; I want their systems to work that way.

Generally, I find that a lot of people use words and terms without knowing what they mean; they're sort of hiding behind their own talk. My Ph.D. is in applied mathematics. My advisor used to say, "If you can't explain it, you don't know it." If you can't put it in regular, simple language that people can understand, then you don't really know what you're talking about.

The great thirteenth-century Japanese Zen master Eihei Dogen talked about *dotoku*, which means *the way of expression*. *Do* is *Tao*, the *way*, and *toku* is *expression*. The way of expression is to express yourself so that somebody can really understand. It goes even further than words; in fact, it doesn't have to be verbal. It can be an emotion, a slap, a sudden, great laugh, it can be anything.

Would it be correct to say that an actor empties himself of his own identity to let the role come through, while a movie star relies more on being sexy or charismatic? The two are very different. So when you say, *That person's an actor*, you perceive him as coming from his whole body and embodying that emptiness.

JEFF: When I make a movie, I often do something to create my own empty space. I'll give you an example. Say I come in, I do all my due diligence, study my lines, think about how to play the character, and feel I'm really ready. But now the other actor is not doing it how I imagined in my hotel room, or the director seems kind of pissed, or it's raining though it's supposed to be sunny in the scene. So I'm starting to feel tight, you know?

So what I sometimes do is start singing or do somersaults around the stage, do something that's apparently inappropriate. I'll scream, get over on my back and just let it rip. Once, I led the cast and crew in a big *om* session. They all chanted this weird syllable: *Ommmm!* And it shifted the vibe; it changed the tightness to looseness. When you do the unexpected, everyone starts wondering what else can happen. They start reassessing all the givens of that moment.

What's great about movies is that all of this is totally allowed; it's even encouraged. Creativity is what's called for. The idea is to get empty so the thing can come through you, you know? What I try to go for is that thing you're talking about, *The Dude is not in.* I'm taking advantage of everything and letting it rip.

It's a little like what you do when you put that nose on. You're doing something unexpected, shattering the boundaries that people assume are there: *What, a Zen master is acting like a clown?* It's also an important reminder to yourself: *All this is nothing but space to be danced in. There's no need to feel harnessed or limited in any way.*

Letting go and emptying myself is such a strong force for me—almost like gravity—that it does me, I don't do it. When the Dude is not in, life just blossoms.

BERNIE: Shakyamuni Buddha said that everything and everyone, as they are, are enlightened. On the other hand, the founder of the Japanese tantric Shingon school, Kobo-Daishi, said that the way you can tell the depth of a person's enlightenment, how much she or he realizes the oneness of life, is by how she or he serves others. So the one who's always in, the one who thinks exclusively of herself, is only seeing the oneness of her own self and that's whom she's going to serve. If what's in is her family and her, then she sees their oneness and that's whom she's going to serve; the depth of her enlightenment is her family. If you see people serving society, the depth of their enlightenment is society. I always point to the Dalai Lama as somebody who's serving the world, not just himself or even his own Tibetan nation. So the depth of his enlightenment is the world, meaning that he sees himself as the world and the world as himself.

To say that someone is completely not in represents an extreme case of a person who has totally let go of attachment to his or her identity. That's a state that none of us is really going to achieve, except sometimes, like during that scream that you mentioned. During that scream there is nothing. Nobody's in.

JEFF: My album, *Be Here Soon*, was a takeoff on Ram Dass's book *Be Here Now*. I thought that nobody would get the title so I kept trying to drop it, but it kept on coming back. The title comes from lyrics in a song, "I'll Be Here Soon," which is a little paradoxical. I mean, don't those words imply that you're already here?

BERNIE: People hear that the practice is to live in the now, and they feel like a failure that they can't do that. I give lots of talks, and almost always at the end somebody raises his hand and says, *You know, I've been trying to practice this for so long, and I still can't be here now.* At that point I always say, *Whoever is not here now, please stand up.* Of course, nobody stands up because we're all here now. Where else can we be?

JEFF: I have to admit that I've had the same feeling as that student. *Be here now. Okay, but I'm not feeling like I'm here right now. I'm feeling like I'll be here soon.* In some way, my saying that I'm not here now feels sort of like an acknowledgment that I am here now, only feeling that I'm not.

BERNIE: "The Dude is not in, leave a message." That's our life again. We're not in, and everybody's leaving messages. Not being in—not being attached to Jeff or Bernie or whoever you are—is the essence of Zen. When we're not attached to our identity, it allows all the messages of the world to come in and be heard. When we're not in, creation can happen.

JEFF: It can have its way, man.

The Dude does his best to take it easy. And that brings to mind going with the grain. When I think of Lily, my goddaughter, I think of the first syllable of her name, *Li*. In Chinese, that literally means the veins of a leaf, the grain in wood or in marble. I did a scene in *Surf's Up* where I'm trying to give a lesson about going with the grain while making a surfboard. You come across a knot, so where's the grain in the knot? Where's the path of least resistance?

BERNIE: When you do judo, you're working with the energy of the person. If you want to go in a certain direction, you wait until the energy of the other person goes that way, too. If it doesn't, you wait awhile, knowing that change happens. As the Dude says, *New shit comes to light,* and when it does, you'll pick it up again. We wait for the grain to go in the direction we want to go, and then we move with it. But new shit keeps coming to light, things keep on changing, and we run into another knot in the wood. So we wait again. We have a little patience.

In 1980 I wanted to build an interfaith community, but there was resistance from different people. It didn't flow, so I stopped and waited. Ten years later it came more naturally and we flowed right with it. That happens all the time; otherwise, you just bully it out and you end up hurting yourself and others.

Some people ask, how long do you wait? Maybe five lifetimes, maybe ten, I don't know. We have to think big.

JEFF: Don't abandon it. Keep it burning.

BERNIE: The grains in the flow of life are always there. At certain times there are unexpected knots, but the grains are still there. One of the key messages of Shakyamuni Buddha was that everything is change. That's why the phrase *New shit has come to light* is so important. Eihei Dogen wrote a treatise called *Genjo Koan* (*Actualizing the Fundamental Point*), which is all about how we live this life in its essence, as both *The Dude is not in* and *The Dude abides*. Toward the end, he adds: "Beyond this, there are further implications." No matter how hard we practice and how strongly we feel that we've mastered our life, new shit will keep coming to light. The situation will change as often as every split moment, and we will find a way to flow with the grain instead of fighting it.

JEFF: When you start opening your heart, the world responds. There is such a need for open hearts that the world will challenge you: *Come on, how much are you willing to give?*

Isn't it the underachiever's manifesto not to be the highest blade of grass because life is just going to cut you down?

BERNIE: In Japan there's a phrase that says that the higher a tree grows, the more wind it has on it. It's a natural part of what it means to grow. You could try to force the wind to stop, but you could also work with it, just like you do in sailing. Be patient; let the circumstances take you there. Go with the wind, and you're either going to get there or you'll get somewhere else.

JEFF: But I sometimes fear my own excitement. Excitement and creativity are wonderful things: *Open, open, do, do!* But the other side is saying, *You might be writing checks that your ass can't cash, buddy.* That's the reason for *Take 'er easy,* because I can get too excited. This is another reason why my wife, Sue, is so good for me. She dampens my excitement in the most beautiful way.

BERNIE: When you talk about the highest blade of grass getting cut, or that life snuffs out those who reach too high, I often think about how true that is for people who try to change the system. For example, take Mother Teresa. She worked hard all her life to make things better for the poor and we all loved her. But she wasn't trying to change the system; if anything, she took care of the fallout from the system, the people whom the system ignored, like the poor and the dying. On the other hand, Martin Luther King Jr. tried to change the system itself. He started out being a spokesman for African-Americans, but he ended up talking against the Vietnam War and the social inequalities in our country—against the entire system—and he got killed. Not everybody is ready to stand up like that because it's dangerous; no system wants to be changed.

Primo Levi, who wrote about his survival at Auschwitz, described Elias, a dwarf who was interned in the Auschwitz concentration camp during World War II. He was enormously strong, bestial, and quite insane, and with those qualities he not only navigated the Auschwitz system, where so many died all around him, but actually thrived. He ate, stole, and seemed quite happy. It was clear that in the world outside Auschwitz, which is a different system, he'd survive only on the outermost fringes of society, maybe even get put away in an insane asylum. But in the system called Auschwitz, Elias was a master player.

So each system forces us to play in certain ways, and you have to look not only at what it's doing but also at what it forces you to do. We have the capacity to sail in any system; we also have the capacity to try to change it. That's the dangerous way to go, because we're going to be criticized, rejected, excommunicated, and maybe even killed.

Lenny Bruce tried to change the system, in his way.

He was a stand-up comedian who not only ranted *about* the system—the system could deal with that—but would also improvise, use obscenities, talk about sex, and say things even he didn't expect to say. That kind of unconstraint and freedom scares people.

My friend the clown and activist Wavy Gravy also tries to change the system, but in a very different style from Lenny Bruce. Wavy once told me he was picketing against the nuclear work at the Livermore National Laboratory in California. The police came to break up the sit-in and he was in a Santa Claus clown costume. They grabbed him, took off his Santa Claus costume, and beat the shit out of him.

JEFF: That's the power of the clown, right? They couldn't beat him up with the costume on. Humor is very good grease, man. Richard Pryor was another guy like that.

But I wonder: Were they trying to change the system, or were they just being naturally themselves? Maybe all Pryor wanted to do was just be who and what he was. It's almost like you can't help it, that's how you address life and the universe; it's who you become.

Maybe you even get addicted to that identity. So are you doing it or is it doing you? Is it even a matter of choice? Do the circumstances bring forth the guy or gal who wants to change the system, or is it the guy or gal who decides to change the system?

BERNIE: Everything is interconnected. Take a forest, for example. It has a redwood that grows ten feet a year and an oak tree that grows one inch a year. There are also circumstances like sun, rain, and soil. But the circumstances include the characteristics of each particular tree. One is going to grow ten feet a year, and one's going to grow one inch a year. Our body's like that, too. Due to circumstances, the hands do certain things and the feet do something else. They share the same environment, they share the same body, but at the same time each has its own aspects.

Nuclear energy appeared, and somebody like Wavy Gravy responded by doing antinuclear work. Much earlier, nuclear energy appeared and the scientist Richard Feynman responded by helping to produce the atom bomb. Both people shared similar circumstances, but they had different personal characteristics, so the result is different. And part of the game also is that Feynman got honors and medals while Wavy gets beaten up by a policeman after he takes off his Santa Claus suit.

There are the Feynmans, the Pryors, the Gravys, and the Bruces. There are the Bridges and the Glassmans. This garden called *us* is a wonderful mixture of totally different trees, plants, and flowers. All of them are different aspects of ourselves, so why kill them or beat them? Why not honor them instead?

THAT RUG REALLY TIED

the

ROOM TOGETHER,

DID IT NOT?

7.

YOU KNOW, DUDE, I MYSELF

DABBLED IN PACIFISM AT ONE

POINT. NOT IN 'NAM,

OF COURSE.

JEFF: Years ago I asked you this question. If the world is one body, what about all the violence we see around us? What about the war and the fighting? If the other shore is right under our feet and everything's perfect the way it is, what is all the killing about?

And it's not just about competing people or countries, it's also competing ideas. During the Holocaust the Nazis didn't want to just wipe out Jews, Gypsies, and others, they also wanted to destroy their ideas and culture. Remember how we talked about the hen and the egg? The hen may think she's pretty important, but all she may be is just another way to make eggs. Again, are you living life, or is life living you?

BERNIE: If we're only here as an engine to move life forward, it certainly affects our sense of our own importance.

JEFF: Have you ever looked underwater at sea anemones? They don't seem to move at all. But if you look at them again using time-lapse photography, you see them pushing against each other, like: *Get outta here! This is my rock, my survival.* Not only do people do the same thing, ideas do that, too.

I don't like all this fighting and killing, I want

peace. You might think it would be wonderful if we could go in and extract all the evil people out of this world, like we extract cancer out of a body. But as Solzhenitsyn says, evil runs through all of our hearts, and who wants to cut out a piece of her own heart? We are part of nature and nature uses violence and war to make its blade sharper and sharper. Life becomes more intelligent, but we only see that after the fact.

When we experience the fighting up close, we don't understand it; we think it's horrible and destructive. Time passes, enabling us to step back, and we get a different perspective. We step out even further back and now there's order instead of disorder.

It's like looking closely at a blood cell through a microscope. Unless you know it's a blood cell, all you see is chaos. You step back, look at it through a wider lens that captures the entire cell, and you say, *Oh, I see, it's a cell.* You look at it through an even wider lens and you say, *Cells are fighting other cells all the time. There's a war going on there!* There are also germs, viruses, and bacteria, lots of things like that, all trying and fighting to live. And why not? I mean, germs have a right to live, too, right? But when you look through an even wider lens you see that all these cells make up your body, and it's one body. And it hits you that you want those battles to go on, because if they didn't, your body would probably not go on living. You look again through a wider lens and you see one body fighting another, but an even wider lens—like history, maybe—shows you something else: *Oh, that's this whole constellation of relationships.* Even wider: *It's all one thing.*

Or you can go the other way, looking at life through greater and greater magnification, revealing finer and finer components. So you're dividing and dividing, trying to figure out who's right, who's wrong, breaking life down even more, and you know what you find in the end? Space.

So depending on how far or how close you get to something, the perspective changes.

BERNIE: You might say that the Buddha had the widest lens of all when he said that everything is one, and that everything is enlightened exactly as it is. But another way of talking about it is connecting it once again to our body. From the Buddha's lens, you're Jeff. He's not that interested in all the pieces that make up Jeff, like your legs, hands, veins, or arteries. He sees it's all one, all Jeff. If you look at Jeff through greater magnification, there are lots of blood cells destroying other blood cells, synapses, membranes, and bones, and they can all look chaotic and even violent. There are desires and attachments, nerve impulses rushing up to the brain and then back down to tell the rest of the body what to do. There's a lot of action there. But if you use a wide lens, it's all one thing, and that one thing is Jeff.

In the same way, if you look at life with the lens of a newspaper, what you'll see is the same competition, action, and conflict. You'll see a country called North Korea fighting another country called South Korea; you'll see floods in Pakistan, the Arctic melting, and politicians arguing. But if you look at it with a wide lens, it's all one, and that's what we call enlightenment. Only you can't just look at oneness, you have to actually experience it, really grok it, not just read, think about, or understand it. And the life you live out of that experience we call an enlightened, or awakened, life.

Jeff's body is one whether all the cells and pieces that make up Jeff realize it or not; in the same way, we are all one and interdependent whether we actually realize it or not. But it's nice to experience it, because then we can bring our actions into congruence with what's real, and what's real is that everything is one. When we see that, we begin to treat everyone and everything as one. But in order to see it, we have to practice.

The Bodhisattva sees that there is no separate self and that everything is one, but in order to fulfill his vow to free all beings, he will work with all the pieces. He will recognize Jeff as separate from Bernie, Sue, or Eve and work with him as a separate entity. That means that he's purposely working in the world of delusion, but he's doing this to fulfill his vow rather than to serve his ego.

JEFF: And yet, we have this dream of peace. Is that unnatural?

BERNIE: For me it's utopia, and I don't believe in utopias.

JEFF: Do you believe in peace?

BERNIE: I believe in working toward peace. I believe in trying to reduce suffering. One kind of suffering comes out of people fighting and killing each other, and I've worked a little in that area. But I don't believe I'll ever reach peace if what's meant by that is that no one will ever fight or kill.

Take my body again, for example. I feel my body's at peace, but does that mean that I want my white blood cells to stop attacking the cancer cells in my body? No, sir. For me, being at peace means I'm interconnected. That doesn't mean that blood cells don't engage with other cells, and it doesn't guarantee that cancer cells won't rise up and take over my body one day. That's the flow of life, and it won't stop whether we find a cure for cancer or not. If I can somehow take a leap and see the workings of the whole universe, I'll see lots of things that are not at peace with others. Wolves attack sheep, weeds kill flowers; that's life. I've worked all my years to reduce suffering, but I don't try to change the wolves or the weeds.

JEFF: The name of your organization is Zen Peacemakers, right? So when you say making peace, what are you making, exactly?

BERNIE: I'm Buddhist, but as you know, I'm also Jewish. The Hebrew word for peace is *shalom*. Many people know that word, but what they may not know is that the root of *shalom* is *shalem*, which means *whole*. To make something *shalem*, to make peace, is to make whole. There's a Jewish mystical tradition that at the time of the Creation, God's light filled a cup, but the light was so strong that the cup shattered into fragments scattered throughout the universe. And the role of the righteous person, the mensch, is to bring the fragments back and connect them to restore the cup. That's what I mean by peace. For me, peace means whole. The Hebrew *oseh shalom* is "peacemaker," as in the verse "Blessed are the peacemakers, for they shall inherit the Earth." They shall work to restore the fragments into a whole. And in Zen, as you know, our practice is to realize that wholeness and interconnectedness of life.

JEFF: Wholeness reminds me of the word *context*. President Obama declared that by 2015 we're going to end childhood hunger. In doing that, he created a context, a national agreement that childhood hunger has no place in our country. So the question now becomes, how are we going to do it? By providing the context, the general agreement, he gets us basically on the same team. That means that while we can still argue, there's a sense that we're all in this together. You start intercourse, man, you make love with each other in all the different forms.

It's similar to what John Kennedy did, when he said in ten years we are going to put a man on the moon. You were in that biz of putting a man on the moon, right?* There must have been all kinds of disagreements on the kind of rocket, the fuel, how we were going to do it. But once the context was created—*we're putting a man on the moon*—then those disagreements became a good thing, because now we were working together. Everyone had their own theories, testing them, arguing and discussing, all in an effort to figure out the best way to get to the moon.

BERNIE: It's like the Dude's rug that tied the room together. A bunch of thugs peed on it, but in the end that's still the rug that tied the room together.

---

* Bernie Glassman was an aeronautical engineer who worked in the 1960s and 1970s on designing manned missions to Mars.

JEFF: You know what this also reminds me of? The characters in *The Honeymooners*. We already talked about Ralph and Norton earlier, but there were also Alice and Trixie. Each of them separately was not so interesting. Ralph Kramden was the bus driver full of dreams about how to become more successful; he was also a bully. Alice, his wife, was commonsensical, flat, and down-to-earth. His friend, Norton, was good-natured but simple-minded, and Trixie, Norton's wife, was kind of ordinary and a little bossy. Alone, they were not interesting, but when the four of them came together every week for thirty-nine weeks, they were terrific and millions of people tuned in to see them. *The Honeymooners*, with its stories and situations, provided the context where those four very different characters all worked together, and that changed everything.

I hope that the context of ending childhood hunger by 2015 will transcend the strong political divisions in our country. In fact, that's what motivated me to speak at both Republican and Democratic conventions last summer. Let me tell you that story.

I was finishing a film and looking forward to stopping for a while and spending more time with my family, when Billy Shore, founder of Share Our Strength, asked me to go to the two conventions and talk to the state governors of both parties about Share Our Strength's No Kid Hungry campaign. No Kid Hungry connects children and their families to nutrition programs created by local partnerships of government, nonprofits, and businesses. Many states, Republican and Democrat, are already part of the campaign and we're trying to enlist more.

Now, you'd think an actor wouldn't be that uptight about giving a speech, especially about something he cares about. But I get anxious; I want to do a good job. So I start learning my lines just like I do when I make a movie. I work with Billy, Jerry Michaud, my partner in my hunger work, and others to write the speech, which turns out to be four pages long. Being an actor, I look at it like a monologue I've got to do in a movie, only unlike the movies you don't get a number of takes. You've got just one shot to pull the thing off. So I have some serious anxiety during the two months before the Republican Convention.

We arrive in Tampa. The meeting with the Republican governors is scheduled for 10:30 at night at the end of the convention, which seems to me to be a strange time to be talking to them, but they say that that's the way these things go. We drive to see where the meeting with the governors is going to be, and it's a bar. I'm thinking there will be drinks and music and everybody's going to be drunk. I also have to give the speech a second time at a No Kid Hungry party afterward. I go check that venue and it's a bowling alley.

My talk with the governors gets postponed to eleven, then midnight. By now I'm feeling like a ship, you know? *God, I'll go wherever you take me.* Finally both talks are combined to take place at the bowling alley.

Virginia governor Bob McDonnell, who is chairman of the Republican Governors Association and already part of the No Kid Hungry campaign, arrives, gives me a wonderful introduction, and splits. It turns out that there are no other governors there at all. I end up giving the talk I'd agonized over for two months to an audience of seventy-five college girls at the bowling alley bar. And I don't change a thing, either. I memorized my lines so well that I just give the entire four-page speech written for state governors—*I hope you'll join Governor McDonnell and others to develop state solutions to childhood hunger*—to a bunch of college girls.

BERNIE: Did you bring your nose with you?

JEFF: Damn, I did and I forgot to use it.

BERNIE: Not-nosing, man.

JEFF: Right.

And the Democratic Convention, a week later, wasn't much better. In addition to advocating for No Kid Hungry, I also did a concert with my band, The Abiders, playing for a few thousand people on an outdoor stage. We're about three or four songs into the show when the sky opens up and it starts pouring, with lots of thunder and lightning. I see my brother, Beau, out in the audience, so I call him on to the stage and tell him we have to do a rain dance to stop the rain. So I'm doing these elegant tai chi moves while Beau starts hopping up and down and waggling his hands and elbows like a rooster, only now it's raining and thundering even harder, so I tell him, "No . . . no . . . you're dancing the wrong steps, man—reverse your power . . . you're making the storm worse!" Finally we had to pull the plug, stop the concert. We didn't want to electrify our asses.

It's funny, all the goals I had in mind for the conventions didn't work, but other, unexpected things happened. Isn't that the way it always is? For instance, I'm hanging with a few folks at the Democratic Convention a week later when two kids—about eight and ten, I think—come up to me, looking like little businessmen, and say, "We're entertainers." They hand me their business card and ask me how they could get involved. It was perfect timing, because we're trying to start a youth task force for No Kid Hungry and get young people fired up about it. Kids, you know, have no political representation. We generated a lot of positive media attention for the campaign, too. And, who knows, maybe one of those college girls will be instrumental in ending hunger in her state. You never know how things are affected by what you do.

Whether it's Democrats or Republicans, liberals or conservatives, everyone is a part of the whole deal, we can't do without them.

I think we're slowly moving in the right direction. The planet realizes we have to join forces. That's not going to get rid of all the disagreements and the fighting, but I hope there'll be more experience of context, of wholeness.

BERNIE: One of my goals is to work toward that kind of realization. I also have no expectation of seeing it. For example, who can find anything wrong with *No Kid Hungry in 2015*, which you're working on? Many people from both parties have joined the campaign, but there are some who may say, *If you, a liberal, espouse that, then there's no way that I, a conservative, will agree with you.*

That's what I mean by fragments. Even when people see the value of something, the desire to keep their identity as a conservative, a liberal, or anything else can be stronger than their sense of interconnectedness—even if it means that kids go hungry. *How can I work with a liberal, even if we have the same goals?* It makes no sense, but the differences can take over. That's what we fight wars about.

So we choose the spheres of life where we want to work to change this consciousness. Some of us may feel it's enough just to work with ourselves or our families and not get involved with the rest of the world. But

Buddhism has another practice, which is to work with all those whom we consider enemies and make them allies. If I look at a table as a circle of life, I want to bring everybody to the table to discuss the issues that affect all of us. I'll learn a lot more from working with my former enemies than if I just hang with my friends. My former enemies will learn more, too, and together we'll create a better scene.

JEFF: Creating that better scene doesn't happen in one fell stroke. When we were writing up the Constitution, we put the question of slavery aside because there was too much disagreement about it. The result was that less than a hundred years later we had to fight the Civil War over it. By initially suppressing the issue, we were able to take the first steps toward creating this nation, but we finally had to deal with it because freedom is such a basic right. Long after the Civil War, racism is still with us and may be the main obstacle to our finally all coming together.

BERNIE: Something may look like it's gone for a minute, five minutes, a hundred years, two hundred years, but eventually it will pop up again. If you're not working with the whole picture, if there are pieces you're excluding, it'll come back. Speaking of running into knots and the patience they require, you've been doing your hunger work for some thirty years; I've worked with people living in poverty for that same time. For one reason or another, we've run into all kinds of knots over those years and we had to wait. But I hope that now the environment's different and we can flow again.

JEFF: President Obama's family actually used food stamps when he was a boy; I think that's a first. So new shit has come to light.

BERNIE: And obviously, we both want to invite everybody in. You know, when you feed people and provide community, you're also providing family stability. The rules that were set up for working with the homeless actually break the family apart rather than keep it together. Food is one of the most basic needs of all, because we've all got to eat every day. We need housing, but we need food even more. I don't care who you are, if you starve long enough, you won't act so cool.

JEFF: Hunger has gotten really bad in this country, but maybe this had to happen before people finally reacted. There's no bad that doesn't create some good.

Again, it's like those Lojong teachings that the knots in your life can also be the keys to your liberation. A little adjustment changes the whole damn thing. That's a different way of looking at those bumps—not as barriers but as inspirations, even callings: *Come on!*

BERNIE: The Chinese language is made of symbols rather than letters. Their word for *difficulty* consists of two characters, and one of the characters is *opportunity.* Hidden within every difficulty is an opportunity. I've worked a lot in the world of business, and the problems you run into in business become golden opportunities.

JEFF: I've been often asked in interviews, *Why do you do the movies you do, and is there a thread that runs through them?* I initially thought there wasn't, but then I realized that many of my films have the theme of exactly what we're talking about, that what appears to be a drag is actually a wonderful opportunity. One that really comes to mind is called *American Heart*, about a guy getting out of prison and the last thing he wants is to see his fourteen-year-old kid and have to take care of him. He desperately wants to go straight and make something of his life, and he thinks he won't be able to do that if he's burdened with a kid. Of course, it turns out that getting together with his boy and taking care of his needs really show him what life is all about. They give joy and meaning to his life.

Another practice I find interesting is *tonglen*. That's a Tibetan practice that helps us connect with others' suffering and our own. I'm kind of a beginning student of it, but one idea I really like is that your feelings are not just *your* feelings, we all have them. So in some ways, you're a representative of what it is to be alive. As an actor, I feel that I represent a community, the family of man and woman, and my job is to show how different people will act in different situations, like the father in *American Heart*. So when it comes to feelings of struggle and suffering, you're not alone; your suffering is on behalf of the whole group, on behalf of all of us.

That thought alone eases things. It's also the beginning of compassion.

8.

YOU MEAN COITUS?

JEFF: We had a group of guys up here, Alan Kozlowski, John Goodwin, and Chris Pelonis,[*] playing music and doin' a hang, and the discussion turned to A440. *A* is a note in the musical scale above middle C and 440 refers to its frequency, 440 Hz. When musicians tune up together, they use A440 as their standard for setting mu-

---

[*] Cinematographer Alan Kozlowski, songwriter John Goodwin, and acoustical designer and musician Chris Pelonis.

sical pitch. And the discussion was: Is A440 an absolute truth or is it just something arbitrary we use to create the standard? Johnny's point of view was that A440 is a relatively modern standard of tuning and basically it's an arbitrary thing. Pelonis, who is an acoustical engineer, said that A440 is not just the frequency of the note A but is also the earth's vibration. Earth has a basic resonance, and that's why *A* became the standard. He summarized it this way: "The region of 440 is by Supreme design and not arbitary or coincidental."

So is there an ultimate reality? And if there is, how do you know what it is?

BERNIE: In Zen we talk about bearing witness, or being one with something. First you have to be in a space of not-knowing, letting go of attachments to who you think you are, and then you can bear witness to life around you, which means becoming it. And I mentioned that Zen has practices to help you do that, like koans.

One of those koans is *Contemplate A*. The first letter in the Sanskrit alphabet is pronounced *Ah*. In the Tantric tradition, *Ah* is the seed syllable of the universe.

So you can expound on Ah or explain Ah, you can even pronounce Ah, but none of these are enough. To work on the koan *Contemplate A*, you have to come into total resonance with Ah, you have to become that vibration, Ah.

The same with the basic resonance of the earth. Let's say you want to tune your life to be in resonance with the earth, just like you want to tune your guitar to be in resonance with the rest of the band. You don't talk about A440, you play it. Similarly, you don't talk about the resonance of the earth, you become it. The resonance of the earth was there before anyone knew about A440, so how do you be that? Leaves turning, flowers popping open, rain falling on a leaf, the leaf bending under the weight of the raindrop, and the raindrop hitting the ground—these are all resonances of the earth. How are you in resonance with them?

I can say, "Birds are flying in the sky." Those are words I've learned. If you didn't know the word *bird*, what would you call it? When the first ships came to America, the natives didn't see them as ships because they had no word for *ship*. What they saw were new patterns; they didn't call it this or that.

Once we have words, we get stuck to them, especially to what we think they mean. Don't forget, a word may mean different things to different people. I've heard that the Eskimos have ten words for snow. They may say, *It's such and such*, and people who're not of their culture won't understand, because they don't experience snow like the Eskimos do. But if you pick up a handful of snow and put it against somebody's cheek, she experiences snow; she doesn't need the word.

Words are important because they give us a way of informing and dialoguing with each other, but they don't necessarily help us experience the thing itself. You can't use words to experience an apple, you taste it. To experience life, you can't just give out names, like *A440, resonance of the earth, apple, snow, enlightenment*, whatever. It's the experience that counts.

JEFF: Didn't you mention that the *Heart Sutra*, which is a famous sutra in Mahayana Buddhism, begins with the letter *A*, as in *Avalokitesvara Bodhisattva*,* and that

---

* Avalokitesvara Bodhisattva, doing deep prajna paramita, perceived the emptiness of all five conditions and was freed of pain.

you could sum up the entire *Heart Sutra* in that one letter?

BERNIE: Yes, but again, not just by reading A. You have to become one with it, plunge into A, and then you're at one with the whole sutra. That sutra talks about the state of not knowing, so if you're at one with the sutra you're in resonance with the entire universe. Of course, we are always in resonance with the entire universe because we *are* that universe. But how do we become aware of it? How do we experience it? By getting into that space where that's *all* we experience, where there's nothing but A.

Isn't that what happens in acting? Somebody plays a role. He does everything right but you don't feel that he really embodies the character. It's got nothing to do with the words or even with what he's doing, it's something deeper. It's that extra step that I believe makes a great actor. He's bearing witness, he's embodying; there's no subject-object separation. If there is, he can speak the lines and go through all the right motions, but there's that extra little thing, that layer of separation, that the audience can feel. It's the same with a great speaker. You go to a lecture, the speaker is fantastic, but you know there's something not real about it. He's talking about things he hasn't borne witness to, hasn't lived. That's the extra step that we try to get you to take in koan study.

JEFF: One of my favorite actors is Tommy Lee Jones. He brings an intensity to his characters that is so rich and mysterious. He's very opaque; you don't see all the wheels turning, which I admire in actors. To me it seems more the way people act in real life. I don't particularly care for the kind of actors who feel obligated to show you everything; that's what we mean by *indicating*. They're going to show you what they think the audience needs to see, to tell the story. But with Tommy, like a lot of other actors, you don't see the work. You don't see the practice, the effort; he's not trying to do anything, he's just there.

BERNIE: There was this wonderful ninth-century Chinese Zen master, Zhaozhou. He trained for forty years with his teacher, and when he finished his studies he said, *I'm going to go on the road, and if I run into an eight-year-old girl who embodies this path, I'll stay and learn from her. And if I run into an eighty-year-old master who's got all of the answers, I'll move on.* He didn't want answers, he wanted the life. So he went out searching for people who were just people, who really had embodied living this life fully, in the moment.

JEFF: When I make a movie, I attempt to get deep as quickly as I can with the guys I'm working with, both the cast and the production crew. I don't even do it consciously anymore, because it's become second nature to me. I want to get as deeply connected as possible with the director so that we can become almost like different impulses in the same brain. That intimacy is the snake I referred to earlier. The final movie is the snakeskin, which is nice by itself, only it's not the snake.

The most important thing is to exercise this closeness we have together. It's a chance to overcome resistance to birth, opening, growth, and life. Coitus, man. Making a movie is just the place to do it, like a church is the place to pray. It provides the safe, generous space to cook in. We've got all these artists together working to make something very special in two or three months, maybe six, that's it.

So the intimacy you develop on a movie set is really something. Most movies—and stories, for that matter—have something to do with love, you know? When you do a love scene with somebody, loving becomes so accessible and easy, especially when two people are doing it on purpose, really opening their hearts. That's why people fall in love with their costars. Then they make the misstep of fucking and that can screw it all up. My wife, Sue, is my leading lady in the real movie. We've just celebrated our thirty-fifth wedding anniversary and our relationship is the most precious thing to me. But that doesn't close down my intimacy with other people. If anything, it makes me love Sue all the more. The freedom that she gives me, loving me as I am, causes me to want to get closer and closer to her all the time and inspires me to give her that same freedom. We practice our love.

Practice, man. That's what scratches my itch. It's like when I'm making a movie. Each time I have the same kind of panicky feeling in the beginning: *Am I gonna be able to pull it off? Am I gonna be prepared? Am I gonna be able to do what's called for?* And every time I prepare, I feel much better.

BERNIE: We have to practice in order to experience being in tune with what's going on. When you play your guitar with your band, everybody's instruments have to get in tune using the same frequency; everybody has to get in resonance. That requires a common intention.

JEFF: Not only are the instruments in tune, everyone's intentions are also in tune.

BERNIE: But all that's gone once you're playing. You're not thinking anymore, *Hey, I'm in tune with the other guys.* You're just playing and experiencing the resonance.

JEFF: The song is playing you.

BERNIE: There's the phrase *freely playing*, like the phrase *at play in the fields of the Lord*. In that state you're no longer practicing, you're just freely playing. Say the entire group is in that state, and now you're joined by another musician, who comes from a whole different culture than yours with no sense of A440 but with a different tonal scheme instead. If that person joins you, the whole group is going to pick up on it and will play a different song or riff from what it would have played otherwise. That's what happens if you're in the realm of freely playing. If, on the other hand, you're in the realm of practice, and this new musician starts playing, you might think: *Hey, that's weird. Let's stop for a second and figure out what to do.*

In life, it's very important to practice. That's one of the ways that we're going to get in harmony with everything. But the most enjoyable times are when we're just freely playing in the fields of the Lord, in the fields of the Pure Land.

JEFF: What I dig is that it's having its way with us, you know? It's so great when that happens in a movie or any kind of art. The tricky part is getting hooked. The kind of fish I am, I try not to get hooked. That's kind of my approach in life. I have a lot of resistance to getting hooked because I know the engagement and the investment that will be required. And you only have so much time to do things, so once you choose to do one thing you're not going to do others. But once you get hooked and it's pulling you along, a wonderful thing starts happening, where it starts to do you instead of you doing it.

BERNIE: Lovemaking is very similar.

JEFF: Again, coitus, man.

BERNIE: There's foreplay, during which you try to get in resonance with each other, and then there's the time of coitus itself, where you're not doing any of that.

JEFF: It's doing you.

BERNIE: That's playing. The other is practice.

JEFF: There's a very fine line between those two. Can you play and practice at the same time?

BERNIE: We say that the distance between heaven and earth is the breadth of a hair.

JEFF: And you can kind of go back and forth.

BERNIE: You're always going back and forth.

JEFF: I got a one-track mind, man. Coitus keeps coming up. It's wonderful to get in that groove. You can't make a mistake if you wanted to, and neither can the other. It's like what Miles Davis says: "Don't worry about mistakes, there aren't any."

Bernie: We've talked about practice and freely playing, but there are certain people who seem to jump into freely playing without any preparation. How would you relate to people like Sid Caesar or Robin Williams? I heard that Sid Caesar never went by a script, though he always had one. He just reacted to the other people or the situation.

JEFF: I remember watching his show as a kid. And I played with Robin Williams in *The Fisher King*.

When I got the gig I was a little worried, you know: *Robin Williams! He riffs all the time, he can't help it, it's like a tic. I've got this scene in the end where I'm supposed to give this big soliloquy while he's lying there in a coma, and I can imagine him suddenly going, AAAAH, you know, fucking with the scene and with me.* Instead, I got to that scene and his presence was so beautiful. He didn't have anything to say because he was supposed to be in a coma, so he could have gone to sleep while I did my lines. But he was awake and present. He supported me in the most wonderful way without saying one word.

Robin went to Juilliard; he's a trained actor. The way I look at it, comedy's just one of many things he can pull out of his kit bag. When we did *Fisher King*, we'd be working long, sixteen-hour days, it would be four in the morning, and we'd be dragging. All of a sudden Robin would plant his feet and just riff on everybody in the room. He had us all in stitches. It was like jazz, you know. Many directors would laugh a bit and then tell everybody to get back to work. But not Terry Gilliam. Terry would egg him on. He'd have him go on for half an hour or so; Robin would have gone on forever. We were so energized we'd get back to work and have three or four more hours of juice. The power of the clown, man.

BERNIE: Would you say that Robin Williams spends a lot of time in the world of practice, or does he just play?

JEFF: Both, I think. You practice going a little further, making that insult a little sharper. At some point it becomes playing, things come out and you can't help it, it becomes a reflex thing. So he probably goes back and forth. You can practice playing, can't you? I mean, you practice getting into that groove, into that spot. Isn't that meditation?

There's another way of looking at practice. A doctor might say, *I practice surgery.* That's a little bit different, isn't it?

BERNIE: For me, I'm practicing when I'm in a place of no subject-object relationship. I could be working, but if I'm just totally in my work it becomes play.

JEFF: In that instance, practice and play become the same thing, right? In acting, rehearsal might be thought of as a practice. But when I'm rehearsing, that's the time to also really get down and play. Just get into the thing, see where it takes you. As Sidney Lumet said when we were going through *The Morning After* day after day, it's like peeling the onion. Each time you do it you're going to find new things. You practice freshness, practice playing.

BERNIE: So can people just play their life, or do they have to practice their life?

JEFF: Or indicate their life? Or rehearse their life?

BERNIE: In my terminology, if you bear witness, which means you're living it, then you're playing. If you follow your ideas about what you're doing, you're practicing. I like to work with people in their lives, whether at the workplace, their home, whatever. So how do you get them to play their life, to totally plunge in, do what you did with Sidney Lumet, do the whole movie? Say you're doing your life, and now it's changed a bit. You're not stopping every three seconds to say, *Did I do it right? What's a better way of doing it? Did those people do it right? Are they screwing up?* You're just fully living your life. For me, that's play. And I think we can train to do that, and that training is the practice.

My experience is that when you really play your life rather than rehearse it, it's beyond joy and sadness, you just feel much more alive. When you're in a planning mode, all kinds of stuff come up: *I should have done this, I should have done that, why didn't I do that?*

If at some point you decide you want to teach acting, I'm sure you'll teach people to be alive in their acting. That will be a practice. And I think certainly in

Zen or Buddhism in general, the role of the teacher is to try to help a person be alive in their life. And they have to practice.

JEFF: Those knots we were talking about earlier can be invitations to practice. We're busy playing, only now our clown gets knocked over or life hits us in a bad way; those are all reminders to practice.

9

WHAT MAKES A MAN,

MR. LEBOWSKI?

JEFF: Just like in life, there are many paths to acting, many ways to do it. There are some actors who
want you to call them by their character's name. They
don't want any kind of involvement or engagement
with you outside of the role. A lot of great actors are like
that. My school is more like, *I want to know the person in*

real life. I want to know who that person is, and I find that informs the work.

There are two words that mean kind of the same thing, but also different. For instance, there's *hot* and *cool*. There's *Hey man, you're cool!* And there's also *Hey, you're hot, man*. They're both good things, but kind of different. So you'll get someone like Scott Cooper, who directed *Crazy Heart*. He was so encouraging and genuinely excited. Then you get the Coen brothers. They're not particularly demonstrative. They're masters, funnier than hell, but kind of cool. That's their style, you know what I mean?

Movies throw together all these different kinds of people who're trying to do their art and it's all workable. The weirder the approach sometimes, the groovier. Like the bit of sand in the oyster that creates the pearl. If the grain in the wood is perfect, it's not as interesting. When you get a burl, for instance—God, it's wonderful!

BERNIE: I feel fortunate that I was able to study with a wide assortment of teachers, with very different styles and ways of doing things. Then there are others, who warn you that you'll get too scattered, just stay within this niche and work there. But life isn't a niche, life is life. If you just stay in that one little place, how are you going to feel alive? So I like to work with as many different personalities as possible: hot, cool, tepid, whatever. It's exciting.

JEFF: And so endearing. You know, we're all basically the same, wanting to be loved and wanting to love.

You remember that great Marvin Hamlisch song, "What I Did for Love"? It reminds me of the Joy of Singing workshop that I took years ago, run by Warren Lyons. The workshop was two weekends long and the class was made up of opera singers, gas-station attendants, carpenters, anyone who wanted to learn about singing and creativity, because the two are connected. What Warren taught us was that whatever keeps us from going all out in our singing, whatever muscle keeps our song down, also keeps the rest of our creative juices down. This can happen because of something way back in your early life. For an example, maybe in grammar school you didn't sing so well and the teacher said, "Bernie, can you just mouth the words instead of singing them?" From then on some muscle got crippled and you don't sing loud, not even in the shower. This was the muscle Warren wanted us to open up, our creative muscle.

The first weekend, everybody had to stand up alone in front of the class and sing "On a Clear Day," which has incredibly beautiful lyrics but a pretty difficult melody. I sang, too, but I also watched the others. We'd get up there and we would use everything we had because we were on the spot, we had to sing. And when you're in that situation you pull out everything you've ever used in your life to make people love you, whether it's self-deprecation, charm, shyness, whatever. It all comes out.

I learned that it's not about hitting the note sharp or flat. Sinatra would sometimes hit a note a little flat, too, and that imperfection made the sound even stronger. It's not about perfection, it's about authenticity.

Warren assigned each person a song that would bring out something he or she was avoiding in life. There was a banker there, and the song Warren gave him to sing was "What I Did for Love." It fucking broke my heart, man. He got up there nervously and said things like *I can't do this, I'm not a singer, but here I go.* He began to sing barely in tune, struggling, and that struggle was so courageous. We're all doing the best we can, we're pulling out all of the stuff that works and doesn't work in our lives, and how all that shows up in the world is so unique and beautiful.

In the movies you work with all kinds of actors, some sort of gruff or not so easy to get along with. But that's what they do for love. That's what they have to do to be here with us, and it's wonderful. You look at a twisted oak tree and it's beautiful, because it's being what it has to be, which is twisted. Even people who're fighting you or are against you for whatever reason—there's a beauty in everything we do and who we are, you know?

Going back to the music workshop, I noticed that one of the things that got in the way of my song coming out was being afraid of really plugging in. The songs that Warren gave us were the standards, the great show tunes. My wife, Sue, joined me there on the second weekend and we did a wonderful exercise. You had to hold hands with your partner, look into each other's eyes, and sing to each other. The task of the person being sung to was to receive the song. The task for the singer was to give full expression to the song. The song that I was assigned to sing to my wife was "Somewhere," from *West Side Story*, which begins with the words "There's a place for us." Those words are so gorgeous and so deep that when I got in touch with them it was too much; I felt paralyzed. Finally I just let them do what they did to me and managed to sing them through sobs and tears.

The song Sue was to sing to me was "Someday My Prince Will Come." Sue somehow managed to sing her song a little more intelligibly and I remember the love shooting out of her eyes. Strong stuff, you know? Maybe even frightening.

BERNIE: Touching places you're afraid to go to?

JEFF: The feeling is so strong you shut down, almost like it blows out your instrument. You can't sing, speak, or anything.

BERNIE: Like reaching a knot in the wood?

JEFF: Yeah, maybe. When you're a performer, you feel the pressure to get on with it. You have this set amount of time, and if you don't perform you're going to lose your audience. But Warren created this safe place where there was no time limit. You had the space to really be with the song and feel it. When you're making a movie, it's up to the actor to create this kind of safe inner environment, but a director can support that, as if he's telling you that you've got all the time in the world.

I did Hal Ashby's last film, *Eight Million Ways to Die*. My brother Beau had done his first, *The Landlord*, so I'd known Hal for a long time. He was one of my favorite directors, a master. Hal had such art balls and so much faith in the actors he assembled that he gave us lots of freedom to improvise. The script, as far as he was concerned, was just a rough outline of the story; the scenes we shot often had very little to do with the dialogue in the script. Hal used this method in all the movies he made. Look at the pudding that came out of this guy's oven: *Coming Home*, *Being There*, *Harold and Maude*, *Shampoo*, *Bound for Glory*, and *The Last Detail*, among others.

In spite of these great movies, Hal's method of making them drove the producers and financiers crazy. They would see the dailies, the scenes we shot the day before, and say, *What the fuck? These words aren't in the script. He's making a completely different movie from the one we hired him to make.*

When Hal first gave me the script for *Eight Million Ways to Die*, I asked him why he wanted to make this film; it didn't really seem to be the kind of story he'd be interested in telling. He said, "You know, I have the same question. I guess that's why I want to make the movie, to find out why I want to make it."

The producer of this film didn't respect Hal's method. One day, when we had about another week of filming to go, he came and told Hal, "You've got just today and then we're pulling the plug." You can imagine how heartbreaking that is when you've put so much love and energy into a movie and now you're being told that your vision will be badly compromised. Hal took his broken heart into his trailer, probably burned one, for all I know, then came back out with an idea of how to truncate the film schedule and finish the filming by the end of that day.

Now, this was Andy Garcia's first movie. He and I had a great time; the environment Hal created was very inclusive, so we'd all give each other ideas. But now we were under the gun, time was of the essence. Hal had worked out this way of adding more exposition by having Andy do a long telephone conversation. Andy did three or four takes, and I saw there was a problem.

So I went up to Hal and said, "Hal, I think Andy's having a problem with this part of the dialogue. I have an idea."

Hal said, "You know, you're probably right. But Andy's a good actor, let's let him figure it out by himself."

Hal created the alternative reality that we had all the time in the world. Even though we were under such time constraints, there was no panic whatsoever and we got the work done.

In the end, even though he completed the film as instructed, when he gave it to the editor to assemble and took a two-week vacation, the producer came to the editing room, confiscated the negatives, fired Hal, and cut the film with complete disregard for Hal's vision. Seeing that Hal Ashby was an Academy Award–winning editor and such a master filmmaker, this seemed to me like a case of cutting your nose off to spite your face. That was the last movie Hal made and he died shortly afterward.

Hal was such a wonderful cat, I remember him telling Andy and me, *I want to set up a little editing room in Malibu and teach you guys how to edit film; I'd love you to come by and cut some of the scenes with me.* Unfortunately, that never got to happen. Andy and I often reminisce about what a wonderful time we had and how sad we are that Hal wasn't shown the respect that he deserved.

So there is a window where you have to perform, but if you can do that with the feeling that there's no window, that's wonderful. It lets you open up and go deep.

At the same time, there are some things that prevent us from opening, like when I had to sing "Somewhere" to Sue and I was almost paralyzed. For instance, it's cool to be together with someone you love, but what makes me different also has to be respected. I guess I want that same respect and safe space in personal relationships that Hal gave Andy and me and that he didn't get from the producer.

You see it in the history of our country. Before coming together, the thirteen original colonies fought each other before realizing they were going to be stronger and more effective if they joined forces. In feudal times, before there were countries as we know them, cities and towns battled and warred for years before they finally decided to join together to create European states.

BERNIE: People hang on to their separate selves for dear life, afraid to come together. But the one is still much stronger than the pieces.

JEFF: I think this fear of being vulnerable and looking weak accounts for our fear of bearing witness. I love living in the United States, but I can feel the fear. When 9/11 happened, for a short while there, maybe a week or two, everything got very soft. There was a lot of sadness, a lot of loss, and also a lot of compassion. Then what was soft became rigid. We contracted and lost our openness. We got tight: *Dammit, we're going to get them! We're going to make war on terror.* That always seemed absurd to me. We couldn't stay with questions like: What is our place in the world? Why did those guys crash airplanes into our buildings and kill so many people? What had we done, if anything, to get such a reaction?

I'm not a political expert by any means, but I do know that we have supported many dictators and supplied them with guns. But questions like that make us feel too vulnerable and afraid. It was one thing to say that 9/11 was terrible and we had to catch and punish the crazy guys who did it; looking at it as an all-out war was something else. Much of our nation was overcome by fear, and politicians responded: *We've got to protect ourselves so we're going to war.* And if you were a politician who didn't agree with that, you couldn't play the game; many people felt they couldn't speak their minds during those years.

In the same way, we can't fully acknowledge the evil of slavery in our history or how we treated Native Americans and how that goes on even now. So we have to bear witness. We have to own our part in everything because there is nothing that isn't a part of us.

BERNIE: One of the twelve steps of the AA program is to make amends to those you've harmed. It's never too late. So certain people attacked us on 9/11. They were fanatics and most people around the world, including Muslims, were horrified. At the same time, many of those same people felt that we'd acted like big bullies for years. That didn't justify 9/11, it just pointed to the bigger context in which all this happened. So what was the right action? Getting and punishing the criminals, but also bearing witness to what we've done in the world and making amends. That might have changed the situation significantly as opposed to just going to war.

JEFF: But we're afraid of doing things like that because it means opening up and being vulnerable. How many of us are ready to acknowledge the effects of our military-industrial complex, which Eisenhower warned us about so long ago? It's a self-perpetuating machine that makes a lot of money while people can't feed their families or educate their children.

In general, I feel that you've made your whole life about working with people who are suffering, and you invite me to do the same thing: *Come on, you wanna play in this?* And I say, *Yes, that's my game, too.* The invitation to me—from my mom, from Sue, and now from you—is: *Open, open, open.* Without that, nothing gets born. At the same time, giving birth and getting born can get really uncomfortable.

BERNIE: But it's the only game in town. There are lots of reasons why we don't open, apologize, and make amends easily. They're also the reasons why, when we'll finally turn around and take those actions, the effects will be immeasurable.

10.

WHAT DO YOU *DO*,

MR. LEBOWSKI?

JEFF: Remember the movie *The Graduate*? Remember that party scene in the beginning of the movie when Murray Hamilton tells Dustin Hoffman's character, Benjamin, "I just want to say one word to you. Just one word . . . Plastics."

Well, I just recently got turned on to the terribleness of what we do with plastic. I learned about ocean gyres, which are large spirals of currents. There are five gyres in the world's oceans and a couple of them are filled with plastic—bags, bottles, all kinds of stuff. The material is indestructible. We say it's biodegradable, but it's not, it just breaks down into smaller and smaller bits that microscopic animals eat. Fish eat them, then we and the birds eat the fish. We're addicted to these bottles and bags, it's kind of insane. How do we become more aware of that and what can we do about it?

BERNIE: We do what we can do. You came to our Symposium for Western Socially Engaged Buddhism in Massachusetts in the summer of 2010. We didn't buy plastic bottled water, people drank our own delicious well water. If you think about it, there's always something you can do. Saying it's just too much and not doing anything is no answer at all.

What I see again and again is that when we look at what to do in life, we tend to be constrained by what we don't have instead of appreciating what we do have. In my book *Instructions to the Cook*, I emphasize looking at the ingredients you have. So let's say that you and I are going to make breakfast and you've got certain things in the refrigerator. We want to make the best meal that we can make, and we're going to eat it and enjoy it. But imagine that if instead of doing that, we say, *I want chorizo and there's no chorizo here, so I'm not going to have breakfast. Or I want hot oatmeal and there's no oatmeal so I'm not going to eat.* That's what we do in our life. We say, *I don't have enough time so I'm not going to do anything; or I don't have enough money so I'm not going to do anything; or I'm not trained to deal with plastic so I'm not going to do anything; or I don't have enough enlightenment so I'm not going to do anything.*

Instead, we could say, *Okay, I have no chorizo or oatmeal, but I have green peppers, an egg, Cheerios, and Parmesan cheese.* We cook, eat, and appreciate the meal, whereas if we just sit around bitching about all the things we don't have and not eating anything, we'd starve. And that goes for life, too. Look at the ingredients you have, make the best meal possible, and offer it. Don't forget to offer it. If you make the meal just for yourself, you don't get the same pleasure. It could be as simple as saying hello to a homeless person on the streets. Use your ingredients, and take action.

JEFF: You remind me of a guy who passed away, Rozzell Sykes. I met him shortly out of high school. My girlfriend at the time, Kaija Keel, worked at his place on Sunset. He was an artist and he welcomed me, told me I could bring my guitar. So I would play, he would paint, and we'd just have a great art jam. I think he was originally from St. Louis and he created this whole Jamaican persona, talking in poetry in this Jamaican accent. I got the feeling that he'd done that so long that that's who he became. Maybe he found that to be a Jamaican artist was much easier than being a black guy from St. Louis, you know?

He had this place on St. Elmo Drive, in the middle of the so-called ghetto, right off La Brea; I think it used to be Mary Pickford's stable house. He turned that place into a glorious art space, with galleries showing his and other people's art, plants, filling the grounds with gardens. Everything to him was an opportunity to make art. It became a meeting place for the community. He shared his beauty, his meal, and inspired a lot of folks. Rozzell used to say very much what you're saying: *Be your best you, be love*, and he lived his life like that. Work with whatever you have, and make something beautiful.

BERNIE: With the years, I've come to the conclusion that one of the best ways for realizing the interconnectedness, or the oneness, of life is through social action. Many people say that as a good human being, as a good Buddhist, you should be doing that anyway. I say something more. The way to deepen that realization and actualization is to do social action based on our Three Tenets: approaching a situation from not knowing, bearing witness, and then taking loving action.

If you do that, you're going to, little by little, grok the interconnectedness of things. You're out there serving others, who are aspects of yourself. Buddhism, of course, is known for its practice of meditation for the sake of awakening; I think we can awaken through social engagement, too.

JEFF: I was just thinking of Jon Kabat-Zinn[*] and his expression *the full catastrophe*. The whole picture is kind of catastrophic. He also talks a bit about hopelessness, right? There's the hope of reaching some kind of perfect attainment or happiness, and then that goes bust. But hope continues to bubble up, you know?

BERNIE: I have lots of hope. Expectation is the bummer; that's where I get into trouble. As long as hope is without expectation or attachment, there's no problem. For instance, I like to make vows. The first of the Four Great Bodhisattva Vows is: *Beings are numberless, I vow to free them.* That's a pretty big vow and it will cause me to work very hard. The important thing is not to have expectations.

There are things you want to see happen, too, like meeting President Obama's goal that no child will be hungry by 2015. If you were to expect that, it would be a little tricky, because the odds of it happening are still pretty small. But if your hope and energy are

---

* Jon Kabat-Zinn is a professor of medicine who, through his work on mindfulness-based stress reduction, has brought mindfulness into the medical mainstream as a way to help people cope with illness, pain, stress, and anxiety.

strong enough, you're going to work like crazy to get it done. So the loving action is important.

JEFF: And that's the role of the Bodhisattva. But do beings need freeing? If it's all one body doing its thing, what needs freeing?

BERNIE: If you experience yourself as one body, then you're right, there's no problem. The Bodhisattva works in the world of delusion, with people who suffer because they see themselves as separate from others. She vows to awaken not for her own sake, but in order to relieve everyone's suffering. She doesn't sit around smoking a cigar without doing anything. Bodhisattvas, by the way, smoke a lot of cigars,* but they also do things. No matter where you are, to whatever degree of enlightenment that you have, you should do the best you can.

JEFF: Is a mensch sort of a Bodhisattva?

---

* Both the Dude and Bernie Glassman like to smoke cigars.

BERNIE: I think it's exactly the same thing. He's a little like the Dude, his good deeds don't draw any attention. He's a Bodhisattva in hiding, humble and unassuming.

JEFF: One of the things I like to do for my mensch friends is give them a little head to let them know I love them. Whenever I make some kind of pottery piece, I always have a hunk of clay left over, and I let my hands go to town with it without thinking too much. So over the years all these small heads have popped out; they're almost like my dolls. Each has its own aspect, its own little vibe and personality, just like people in the world, and they're all aspects of me. Some look pissed off, some look startled, some look like they're singing. Generally, I give them to people I love. I've given you a little head and you seemed to enjoy it.

BERNIE: Definitely. I call him Charlie and I've taken him to all the places where I work: Brazil, Israel, Palestine, India, Sri Lanka, Rwanda, he's been with me everywhere.

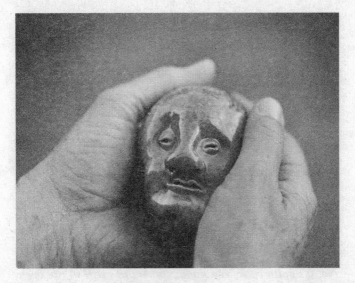

Bernie's head, Charlie.

JEFF: So this thought came to my mind: Why don't I do a project called *Head for Peace* and send these heads out to work for peace?

That set off a whole stream of different feelings and emotions. One said, *Well, yeah, but I don't want these guys to go, I'm really fond of them.* Another said, *Nobody's going to like these heads like I do. They're just hunks of clay, but I've invested a certain something in them.* I don't name them or anything like that, but I put them in my office, they're all over the place, and they like to hang out together. Or maybe I like to put all these different beings, or expressions of humanity, together. So I was split about holding on to these heads or letting them go. When did I first talk to you about this, five or six years ago?

BERNIE: Around nine years ago.

JEFF: And you said, "Let's do it!" But I wasn't ready: *No, it's gotta cook, you know, the bread's still in the oven.* So now, nine years later, I'm ready to pull the bread out. We decided to do this book, *Head for Peace*, with the head that I gave you on the cover.

We both feel that feeding each other and ourselves is a big signpost on the journey toward peace. I've been involved with the movement to end hunger internationally, and more recently in our country, for a long time. You started these Zen Houses and Let All Eat Cafés, so I thought that this Head for Peace project would be a way for us to play together. Each head is for sale with the proceeds going to Zen Peacemakers. It comes resting on a pillow in a nice little box, which also serves as the stand for the head, and can be put on display.

The head sits on your desk, or wherever you want to put it, and somebody might come around and say, *What's that?* And you say, *That's a Head for Peace.* And he says, *What do you mean?* So this gives you the opportunity to talk about your peace work and the Let All Eat Cafés, and hopefully it grows into a whole family of people who want to take care of others. And maybe every couple of years there's an invitation to bring all the heads to one place, because, like I said, they like to hang out together. And people can trade heads or hang out together, just like their heads. It's a work in progress.

Say something about the Let All Eat Cafés.

BERNIE: The Let All Eat Cafés are also a work in progress. Maybe they started in 1991, when I went to live for a while on the streets of the Bowery in New York City, and I invited people to come with me. We ate at different soup kitchens and churches. Some of the churches, usually Baptist, sent out food trucks to reach street people. That's when it hit me that there should be a different-style soup kitchen that will give service with dignity and love.

What do I mean by that? The food, of course, would

be free. *Let them all eat.* But the style of service would be such that you wouldn't be able to tell the difference between poor and rich, homeless and housed. Everybody would eat together. The servers might be the homeless people, those who're underfed, or they might be millionaires volunteering to work in the café.

For example, we had a prototype of a Let All Eat Café in Montague, Massachusetts, which served maybe fifty to a hundred people every Saturday. It was family-oriented, which was very important for me. In the soup kitchens I'd gone to on our street retreats, it was rare to see families with kids. Little by little, I discovered that many families don't want to bring their children there, because they don't feel they're safe, or sometimes they don't want their kids to feel looked down on. I wanted our café to be a place where you want to bring your kids and they want to come. So we had music programs and games, the kids created puppets and did shows and arts and crafts. They went on short hikes into the woods and they also learned how to garden.

The meals were served buffet-style but we put out a menu, and on the back we taped a dollar bill. People were told that they can keep the dollar bill or, if they wished, they could put it in a pot to be used for food for the next meal. My sense is that kids should learn at a young age about money and giving. European cities have a big street scene, with mimes, bands, and all kinds of clowns on the streets. Families walk by, pause to watch, and the parents give their kids a little money to give the entertainers. Kids love to be able to give. That's what I mean by service with dignity, service with love.

Meantime, the adults were offered mindfulness-based stress-reduction programs, counseling, massage, and acupuncture, as well as some medical and dental treatment. An AA meeting took place. The food was nutritious because much of it came from our own organic garden or from other local farms. It was the full monty. That's why we called it a café instead of a soup kitchen, and our goal was to make it a model for cafés across the country. We're now developing something similar in the neighboring city of Greenfield, Massachusetts.

JEFF: Let All Eat.

BERNIE: Somebody once wrote a little note saying, "Thanks for the café. I eat in many soup kitchens, and I really appreciate the food here. But what I appreciate most is that I don't feel needy." That feeling of neediness, of separation between you and someone else, was exactly what I hoped would disappear. We'd like to train more people in this methodology so that more such cafés can arise.

JEFF: It's like bringing everybody to the table, not leaving anyone outside. We're all here on this earth together.

BERNIE: Exactly. If we can get to the moon, we can feed our kids.

JEFF: And we made it to the moon.

11

NOTHING'S FU**ED, DUDE

JEFF: People complain a lot about the notion of instant gratification in our society: *I want this now, I want it this way, and I'm gonna get it, watch me, boom!* But since everything is changing and new shit is always coming to light, we can always learn, right? Let's say someone gets drunk. She wakes up hung over and thinks: *Oh yeah, that wasn't such a good idea.* She learns something.

BERNIE: Unless she likes going unconscious with alcohol and wants to repeat that again and again. If you hang on to the gratification, new shit can't come to light because you're attached to it and will try to repeat it.

The other side of that is someone who wakes up in the morning and thinks, *I can't believe what I did, I'm so screwed up!* If she obsesses over it, that will also keep her in the same place. Either way, she has to let go, and that'll move her toward less suffering. It may not move her closer to some expectation she has, but overall it will move her in the direction of less suffering. That's just my opinion, and it's a driving force for my practice.

JEFF: Shakyamuni Buddha said in the Four Noble Truths* that life is *dukkha*, suffering. Is he saying there's a way to get rid of that entirely?

---

* Among the Buddha's foremost teachings, saying in essence:
    a. life is suffering;
    b. suffering arises from attachment or desire;
    c. suffering ends when attachment or desire ends; and
    d. the way to achieve that is by following the Eightfold Path.

BERNIE: He said there's a cause to suffering and therefore a path out of it, which is described in the last of the Four Noble Truths.

JEFF: Are there people who have ended suffering completely?

BERNIE: I doubt it. When I teach, I encounter all kinds of ideas about delusion and enlightenment. For instance, I tell people to write down the names of all the people who they think are fully enlightened, and on a separate list the names of those they think are deluded. It usually turns out that all the people on the fully enlightened list are people they've never met; often they've been dead for a thousand or two thousand years, like Shakyamuni Buddha, Jesus, Moses, people like that. Whoever they've met and is alive and kicking is usually on the deluded side.

Eihei Dogen said, "Delusion is enlightenment." He meant, this is it, man. It's not like you get to some place where the suffering ends.

JEFF: What's the difference between delusion and illusion?

BERNIE: I used to do magic long ago when my kids were young. I think that when I set something up so that what you see is different from what's really happening, I'm creating some kind of illusion. But delusions are any ideas or concepts that you think are true, anything you're hanging on to.

JEFF: Making movies is full of magic. There are two kinds, really. One is the kind of magic that you're talking about, creating an illusion, like sleight of hand. In movies, that type of magic appears in special effects, makeup, the audience not seeing the fake nose from the real one. But there's another kind, what I call real magic, or alchemy, where all the artists show up, throw their best shit into the pot, and something comes out that no one expected, something that reflects the human experience so deeply and meaningfully that it touches the heart of all those who see it.

Enlightenment is magic.

BERNIE: And there are various depths of it. If I'm attached to this skin-and-bones Bernie, and I think of that as myself, that's a delusion, and whatever I do—my loving actions—will be oriented toward taking care of this bag of bones.

Now I think my family is myself, my community is myself, even the whole universe is myself. These are all deeper levels of enlightenment. But no matter how far I go, even if I realize that the whole universe is me and now I'm working for everyone and everything, there's still a delusion I'm hanging on to, there's some kind of cap I'm putting on who I am. As long as that goes on, I'm in the realm of knowing, which is the realm of delusion.

A rock has its stage of enlightenment; a cockroach has its stage of enlightenment; Hitler had his stage of enlightenment. We have ours, and our Zen practice is to keep working on letting go of delusions and be in the state of not-knowing. That's why we say it's a continuous practice.

As long as you're experiencing yourself as separate from anything else, that's delusion. And as I said before, I've never met the person who doesn't have some sense of separate self, no matter how small. The reality is that you yourself are everything, you are the universe. So delusion is also enlightenment.

But these are just words. It's theoretical, and it'll stay theoretical till I actually experience what I'm talking about. So I can think, *People are killing each other, delusion is everywhere, and that's enlightenment, just like there are cells in my body killing other cells, it's all chaos, and it's still all one body, it's still Bernie.* That's an abstraction; it doesn't feel real till you actually experience it.

JEFF: Delusion and enlightenment are both going on at the same time.

BERNIE: They're two sides of the same coin. Whatever you do is a reflection of the degree to which you are enlightened. You're going to pick up the person who falls in the street because you know that person is you. You're not going to say, *I've fallen, too bad,* and walk on. So your degree of enlightenment will define what you do.

And as you do things, new shit will come to light, you'll be at a new stage of enlightenment, and new practices will be appropriate. So maybe right now you only pick up the person falling down in your street but not someone falling somewhere else, because that person is not your neighbor. Time goes by, new shit comes to light, and you now see that you are not just your neighbor, you are also any person who falls down in the street. You're at a new stage of enlightenment, so your practices and actions will be different. That's why we say that once you cross the river, get rid of the boat. Don't keep on carrying it, because you're in a new place, so what are the appropriate practices now?

All this is not so easy to see, so find a guide or a teacher to bounce off of; it's hard to do it all by yourself. It's good to have somebody who'll be honest with you and point out to you where you're sticking or attached.

The Dalai Lama basically echoes what the Buddha said. He says again and again that everybody wants to reduce suffering; everybody wants love and happiness. Can we come together around that instead of killing each other and watching children starve?

You can think of the Bodhisattva as Don Quixote, the man of La Mancha, who was both deluded and enlightened all at the same time, and his song is "The

Impossible Dream." *Beings are numberless, I vow to free them.*

JEFF: Isn't feeling that you have to free them kind of arrogant?

BERNIE: In some way. I've played with changing that vow to: *Beings are numberless, I vow to serve them.* It sounds less arrogant and more possible. But whether you serve them or free them, you're helping people see that there is no one truth, that everything they believe or that others believe is just an opinion. If people can grok that, they'll be freed.

JEFF: What if somebody has cancer and is in a lot of pain, is that just an opinion? How do they get freed then?

BERNIE: Freeing people has nothing to do with changing what is. Freeing is seeing what is:

"Okay, I have cancer. What do I do?"

"Take chemotherapy."

"That's one opinion. What's another opinion?"

"Talk to a Native American healer and get his medicine."

"That's another opinion. Is there another?"

"I don't want to do any of it. I am ready to die."

Or: "I want to live and I'm ready to try everything."

I had two close friends who both came down with stomach cancer at around the same time. One decided he only wished to work with Eastern medicine, and if that was not successful, he was ready to go. The other was ready to try everything, and he did: radiation and heavy medications, holistic medicine, peyote in South America, everything he heard of.

You can't eliminate sickness or death, but you can greatly reduce the mental suffering if you see that there is no one truth, that they're all opinions you can play and dance with rather than second-guess yourself, your family, or your doctors. So if you think, *I'm going to do the chemotherapy because only chemo will take care of it*, you may run into problems. But if you see it as an opinion that you can choose or not, that's living with a greater degree of freedom.

Either way, I'm not coming out of some fixed truths or falsehoods. They're opinions and I listen to the one that feels right to me. It's the same if it's someone else's cancer rather than mine. If I have some kind of fixed idea—*This is what you have to do!*—then that doesn't help anyone. Instead, if I can say, "My opinion is that you should do this," it loosens up the world. It doesn't get rid of everything; cancer will still happen, wars will happen, whatever. But when they do, how do I take care of them? Expecting that they won't happen isn't taking care, it's just adding more mental pain.

JEFF: Suffering also leads to the birth of compassion. *I'm going through this, and so is he.* Acknowledging that we all go through pain and suffering can be the key that lets you out of prison. Bearing witness to terrible things can point the way to liberation and freedom. A John Goodwin/Bobby Terry tune comes to mind, "What I Didn't Want." You know, *Thank God, He gave me what I didn't want.* Another knot.

I read *The Myth of Sisyphus* by Albert Camus. The gods condemn Sisyphus to push a large, heavy rock up a mountain, and as soon as he gets to the top, the rock rolls down and he has to roll it up again. So he does this useless, endless, frustrating task of rolling the rock up the mountain and seeing it roll down again, day in and day out. That's a terrible life, you know? I mean, if we're going to push the rock up there, then at least let's build a castle or something groovy. If all you do is just work, work, work, what kind of life is that?

But the essence of Camus's book was that Sisyphus was a hero. Instead of just saying, *Oh fuck, what is the use, man*, he finds some interest in the job: *Oh, look at what happened this time! Funny, I never noticed that little shrub before. The rock sure raised a lot of dust this time when it rolled down, wasn't that interesting? Oh, here it goes again. Oh, there it goes. Watch it.*

BERNIE: One of the definitions of the Bodhisattva is that it's the person who climbs up the mountain, gets a spoonful of snow, comes back down, and throws it into a well. Then she goes back up again to get another spoonful. You can ask, what's the value of working so hard to get a little snow and then throw it into a well? And, certainly, what's the value of getting it spoonful by spoonful?

But is one spoonful of snow like another? More poetically, can you see the sun rise for the first time, every time? Can you live this moment like it's the only moment, as if there's nothing else? The movie *Groundhog Day* is a little bit about that.

JEFF: I also think about Viktor Frankl's book *Man's Search for Meaning*, which was about his life in the concentration camps. Some people in that situation became completely selfish and were willing to do anything to survive, but Frankl felt that this was also the place where angels and saints were born. He lived in what most people would say was a hopeless situation, and he decided that within that, he would do his thing. That book had a big impact on me.

Growth happens out of the most terrible things. It's sad that sometimes those lessons have to be learned over and over and over again. It's almost as if we need terrible things to push off of. So out of the Holocaust emerged that promise that we must never let something like that happen again. If we can learn, then there's goodness there. But God, looking at history, we're fucking slow learners, man.

I recently made a movie, *R.I.P.D.*, that had a scene that took place in a meat locker. We were surrounded by cows cut in half, carcasses hung on meat hooks. Frankly, it didn't bother me that much. I thought, *Gee, we've been in here all day and it doesn't smell that bad.* But when I got home, I got an e-mail from a guy who wanted me to participate in a documentary called *Unity*, and it was all about the importance of being a vegan. And he quoted Tolstoy: "As long as there are slaughterhouses, there will be battlefields." And that rang true for me, because that same disrespect we show animals is what we show people whom we vilify and call the enemy. It's the same consciousness, or lack of consciousness.

I dug what the guy was saying, but I felt my participation would be hypocritical because I've always eaten meat. I've always loved a good steak, you know? *I'd like it rare, please, just knock the horns off.* It was a piece of meat, nothing else. Every living thing has to eat to survive, but there are different ways of doing it. The Native Americans used to kill and eat buffalo, but in a ritualized way that emphasized their respect and gratitude to the buffalo for giving up its life to feed them. Not like us. When you see what we do and how we treat the animals, it's inhumane. And the trouble is, we don't want to look; the denial is amazing. The same kind of thing goes into how we treat people and how we treat each other.

His e-mail did inspire me to try a vegan diet for three months. I enjoyed it and did not miss meat at all. But then I got sick in the middle of making a movie and ended up missing almost two weeks of work, and I thought that maybe I needed to eat animal protein. This is just an opinion and it's probably full of shit; my brother Beau has been a vegan for more than nine years, so I'd like to try it out again.

BERNIE: I've met a lot of survivors of the Nazi concentration camps. One man, who died a few years ago, had a particular impact on me. His name was Marian Kolodziej. He was a Catholic Pole who was taken in one of the first transports to Auschwitz, and he survived there until the end. His number was 432, a low, three-digit number that shows how long he was there. He and those first inmates were used to build a lot of the camp.

Once, they were in line for soup and bread, which was all they got to eat. The guy next to him got his bowl of soup, but one of the guards bumped him and the bowl fell. This guy was Jewish and weak, starved like all the rest of them. So Marian shared some of his soup with him. It's hard for us to imagine this kind of generosity. They were all on the edge of death from hunger; it was almost crazy to share your watery soup with someone else. People killed each other for just one piece of bread.

Some time later, Marian was caught making maps of the camp to be smuggled out to the Polish resistance. He was sentenced to be taken out and shot at the Execution Wall. The Nazis, however, were known for their bureaucratic efficiency; the paperwork had to be properly signed and stamped before sentences were carried out. It turned out that the Jewish inmate with whom Marian had shared his soup worked as a filing clerk in that office, and when he saw the paper authorizing Marian's death sentence awaiting signature, he simply slid it under the stack. He kept on doing that again and again, until he finally found the death certificate of someone who'd died, and he arranged the paperwork in such a way that Marian got the dead man's name and escaped being shot. Marian Kolodziej was that person's name, and that's the name Marian kept even after his release from Auschwitz. Later he said that he himself had died there, and that only Marian Kolodziej survived the camp.

After the war he became one of Poland's leading theater set designers, and for fifty years he didn't tell anybody that he had been in Auschwitz. And then, in his early seventies, he had a major stroke and almost died. As he began to slowly recover, he asked his wife to help him down on the floor of the hospital room and give him a sheet of white paper. She held the pencil in his fingers as he began to draw, and what he drew were his memories and impressions of his time at Auschwitz. When he fully recovered, he went back to the camp and stayed on the grounds for six months, bearing witness.

JEFF: He never told his wife that he was there?

BERNIE: Never. He began with small sketches, his wife helping him hold the pencil when he was too weak to hold it himself. Then he put those sketches together into murals. These murals are gigantic and now cover the immense cellar walls of a large Franciscan monastery just outside Oswięcim, the site of the camps. They make the cellar look like a barrack. Some of the murals show hundreds of inmates, skeletons with large heads and eyes, along with terrifying images of death heads and monsters with fangs and claws. The entire exhibit, which is huge, is called *The Labyrinth*. When you walk through it, it feels like you're walking through old camp barracks inhabited by camp inmates, surrounded by terror and suffering.

We've been taking people to see them at all our Auschwitz retreats. Marian was old and lived far away in Gdansk, but he'd come and join our retreats each year and talk with us. We always sat at the old Selection Site by the train tracks, a long walk from the main gate, and he would make his way slowly on his cane, assisted by his wife. Our bearing witness there was so important to him, and hundreds of participants from different countries, young and old, felt deeply connected to him over the years.

What never failed to touch me was that he had no anger. Imagine this cellar that looks like a barrack, surrounded by terrifying murals, the rest of the retreat people stunned into silence—and he had no anger at anybody.

But he did have some sense of shame. Eve asked him about that once, and he told her, "Whenever somebody tried to escape, the Nazis would make all the inmates suffer. Once, someone escaped and they told us to run along a large, circular track without stopping until they caught him. By the time they finally caught him several hours later, more than three hundred people had been killed, trampled to death by those of us who'd run right over them. So how shouldn't I feel shame?" He was part of a humanity that was doing these things to itself. But there was no anger in him; he was full of love.

JEFF: Why do you think that was?

BERNIE: Because he bore witness to the whole thing, including to the Nazi parts in him. He acknowledged that all of that was him, the murderous guards, the sadistic *kapos*—they were all parts of him and of all of us. At some point you have to decide whether you will love humanity or hate it, and he chose to love humanity.

Marian went through a whole transformation because he went from a period of fifty years, when he wouldn't talk about Auschwitz to anyone, to fully bearing witness. In some of his drawings you see the young Marian holding up and helping the old Marian to keep on drawing. Many people say it's great art, but Marian called it his testimony.

He died about a month before our annual Auschwitz retreat, which takes place in November. Before that, he told his beautiful wife, Halina, that he wanted his ashes to be scattered at Birkenau during our retreat. She came with the ashes, accompanied by a few elderly survivors of the camp, and as she stood there overlooking one of the crematorium sites, she said that Marian's dying words to her were, "Where there's love, there's no death."

JEFF: You run across people who went through that experience who are very angry?

BERNIE: Of course.

JEFF: So are there two paths that humans take when they go through something as terrible as that, one of anger and one of no-anger?

BERNIE: There are lots of other feelings as well, especially guilt. Remember the AIDS epidemic when so many people lost their partners? Remember how depressed they got and full of guilt that their partner died instead of them? We did a lot of work with people with AIDS in Yonkers, New York, and saw that very often.

JEFF: My mom and dad had a baby before me, called Gary, who died of sudden infant death syndrome. I was born a year later. I think my mother had tremendous courage to get back up in the saddle and have another child. Many people think about children as their immortality. She said that they're really closer to your mortality. When you have a child, you have another pair of eyes, another heart that you love more than your own, but you have no control over them. So it took a lot of courage for her to invest that much love once again in someone who could die, as Gary did.

She kept a diary since the age of eighteen and wrote there every day of her life. When each of her children turned twenty-one, on our birthday, she wrote out what was in her journal about each of us, in her own hand, and gave it to us. So we each have our own history as seen through our mother's eyes from before our conception.

When she was eighty years old, she assembled the family: "I want to say something to you. I've written you poems every birthday, but I never wrote a birthday poem for Gary. I never gave him anything." At the age of eighty, she was finally sharing the pain and guilt she'd felt all those years. "You'll notice on the mantel, we have Beau's portrait as a child, Jeff's, and Cindy's. And here is a portrait that I had painted of Gary to hang next to his brothers' and his sister's."

So late in her life she was still growing. When she was around ninety she decided to take up Buddhism. My friend Dawa became her teacher. I remember taking her to one of his talks. After he finished speaking, he asked for questions. My mother raised her hand, Dawa called on her, and she shouted at the top of her lungs, "Words, words, words!" And Dawa said, "Yes, exactly, Dorothy."

BERNIE: My mother died when I was seven, from cancer. We were poor; she was an immigrant from Poland, who didn't want to go to doctors, my older sisters told me. By the time she saw a doctor, it was too late. When she finally went to the hospital, I wasn't allowed by the hospital to visit her. My sister would take me there to stand on the sidewalk, and my mother would wave from a window four stories up. She died about three months later at home, and they didn't let me go to the funeral; once again, they said I was too young. So I didn't have the chance to grieve.

My first real grieving was when my wife died many years later. Then I grieved for a full year.

JEFF: Were you grieving for your mom, too, like hitching a ride?

BERNIE: Yes. It was a little strange, to live to the age of fifty-nine and not go through grieving for my mother, who'd died over fifty years earlier. I had already done a lot by then. My wife, too, was now a teacher—we had cofounded the Zen Peacemakers Order—and I had decided that I was going to stop teaching, that it was her time now. I thought I'd finished my work and that maybe I was going to die soon. Instead, it was she who died, just short of the age of fifty-seven.

JEFF: When my father died, I had a lot of grief, but in some way it felt complete. We'd often tell each other how much we loved each other. I can remember a day when we talked about the handing of the baton at a relay race. That's what our relationship was like. We really sensed it, like *I'm going for us; I'm carrying our spirit.* When he died, I cried and mourned him. At the same time, I felt quite clean with him. But as I talk about it now, I wonder if that's entirely true. There may be a level of feeling there through which I'm not ready to go.

I felt something much sharper when my mother left. Was it guilt? I missed her death by about a half hour. I remember her brother walking out of the house and saying, *She's gone,* just as I was coming in to see her. Beau and Cindy were there weeping at her bedside, holding her hands, loving her. But it was hard for me to open right then. The depth of that loss and emotion felt a bit like when I'd done the Joy of Singing workshop and couldn't sing my song to Sue because I was so overwhelmed.

In a way, I'm not sure they've really gone. I feel my parents so strongly here, in myself and in my children. But there's some incompletion there, something not quite hatched. Maybe it never will be hatched, or maybe it is and this is it, this is what the bird looks like.

My mom and I got to read this poem together one night, "The Lanyard," by Billy Collins, who was poet laureate of the United States. The essence of the poem is: *You gave me life, you gave me everything I needed for living, and I went to camp and made you a lanyard.* It's like, how can I possibly repay what you gave me? *And I made you a lanyard, which you took and said, oh, how beautiful.*

ENJOYIN' MY COFFEE

12.

SORRY, I WASN'T LISTENING

JEFF: I fell in love with Montana while making *Thunderbolt and Lightfoot* in 1974, Michael Cimino's first movie. Two years later I did a movie up there with Sam Waterston called *Rancho Deluxe*. We were shooting at a place called Chico Hot Springs. While we were shooting a scene in the hot tub with Sam, Richard Bright, Harry Dean Stanton, and me, I saw this girl. I couldn't take my eyes off her. Not only was she gorgeous but she had two black eyes and a recently broken nose. Something about her beauty and disfigurement kept me riveted. Every time I snuck a peek, she would catch me. After work I got up the courage to ask her: Would you like to go out with me? She said no. I asked her again, she said no, it's a small town, maybe we'll run into each other later. Those words proved to be prophetic and one night in town we danced, and I fell in love.

The next day I had a meeting scheduled with Duane Lindeman, a realtor who was going to show me some property I was interested in, and I invited Sue to come along. That was our official first date. We went to look at a ranch house for sale on the river. It was fallen down, and mosquitoes were all over the place, but it had some kind of charm.

So I'm looking at this place with Sue, and as we're walking around there's this voice in my head: *You are now looking at this house with your future wife.* I thought, *What the fuck? What are you talking about?* And the voice goes on, *This is your wife.* And I'm thinking, *Oh, no, let me outta here.*

But Sue and I got together. In the beginning it was tough. Earlier I talked about autonomy and freedom. I resisted marrying Sue for a long time because I didn't want to lose either. I felt cornered, not by Sue but by myself. I couldn't bear to let the love of my life slip through my fingers, but at the same time I was afraid of declaring: *This is the one!*

I was crazy in love with her, but I thought, *God, is she gonna be the mother of my kids?* I came from such a great mom and didn't know if either Sue or I had that in us. But mostly the issue was losing my freedom, you know, choosing one woman and that's it, you can't screw around, pollinating all the flowers, no more of that. Sue was very clear, and compassionate. She said, "Jeff, I understand your decision, but I'm going back to Montana. We've been together three years now, and if this isn't what you want, I've got to move on." To make a long story short, I finally got up the courage to ask Sue to marry me, with the secret caveat that I could always get a divorce.

Now we cut to the Seven Sacred Pools in Maui, where we went for our honeymoon. We're looking at these gorgeous falls that finally end up in the Pacific Ocean, and as I'm looking at this beautiful scene I'm consumed by the smell of rotten mangoes, thinking: *Oh God, this is terrible. What have I done?* And Sue immediately picks up on my vibe and says, "I can tell you don't want this marriage, let's annul this, this is ridiculous." And I say, "No, no."

I was this pouting asshole for the first three years of our marriage. Thank God I finally got with the program. You close one door, the door to all other women, but you open a door that leads to a long hallway lined with doors. Incredible doors like children, grandchildren, deeper intimacy with the woman you love, and so many other things that would not be available to you without marriage, without the water under the bridge. Marriage to Sue was frightening for me, but there was also the sense of opening my heart. And thank God I went for it.

I've learned so much from Sue. Authenticity comes to mind; she is the real thing, there's nothing contrived. I'm glad she was patient and didn't kick me out for pouting, thinking I'd been cornered into marriage, or whatever my trip was. She points out to me ways that I defeat myself and I do the same for her.

For instance, as I've said before, I'm often frightened of getting involved in a new project. I'll say, "How am I gonna do this?"

And Sue will remind me, "Hey, this is how *you* do

it. You always get like this when you're asked to do something new." And I'll say, "You're right, that's just what I do." And her pointing that out, and me seeing it, is somehow comforting. I realize, *Hey, I have done this before. Do I want to do it any differently? Or do I want to do it the way I always do it? And can I relax in that—not be uptight about being uptight?* Sue shows me another way of looking at things. We open our hearts to each other.

We do have one ancient war that comes up again and again, which basically runs like this: *You don't get it; you just don't get me; you don't know me; you don't understand.* And that's true. I don't entirely know Sue or her perspective, I never will. And she won't know me or where I'm coming from, really, entirely. But as this ancient war rages, with each battle it becomes more apparent that this inability to truly know the other's perspective is what we have in common. Knowing that, we learn to take our differences and opinions not so seriously, we open up. Having fought this out for over thirty-five years, I now find that when the war raises its head again, I feel: *Great, here it is again, now we get to learn how to love each other even more.*

What is marriage? You're setting an overall context: *Okay, we're going to jam. We're going to experience all our stuff, I'm going to get pissed at you and you'll get pissed back, but we'll be in a marriage. We know we'll have tough times, but we're doing it all together.*

BERNIE: You stand side by side with the other person and you tie the two inside legs together. So now each of you has one leg that's free and another that's tied to the other's leg. You're independent because of your one outside leg, but you're also tied together.

Marriage is also like a miniature Indra's net. The Indian god, Indra, hung a wonderful net stretching out infinitely in all directions, with a single glittering jewel in each eye of the net. Each jewel is its own self, and at the same time it reflects all the other jewels in the net. And there are an infinite number of jewels. When we're together with someone, we have our independence, and at the same time our life is our spouse's life, and vice versa. Little by little, by building these ties, we make Indra's net more explicit. We're connected and reflect each other whether we realize it or not, but relationships help us become conscious of it. That's the difference between theory and practice. So marriage is a practice of making two streams of life three.

JEFF: Speaking of marriage, do you snore?

BERNIE: I don't.

JEFF: Not at all? Eve's never complained?

BERNIE: She snores. She's got asthma and all kinds of allergies. And my dog, Bubale, the pit bull, snores. But I don't.

JEFF: I snore a little bit. Sue snores. My mother was a champion snorer. If she'd had some rhythm, got a groove going, that would have been one thing, but she had these uneven snorts punctuated by long pauses, leaving me to wait for the next snort, which never came when I expected it. Trying to sleep next to a snorer is interesting.

On the one hand, you can decide to be with the snoring. On the other hand, you can move elsewhere and find a quieter place to sleep. How do you work with it?

BERNIE: Moving away is working with it.

JEFF: Just get the hell out of Dodge, man. But you can apply that to other uncomfortable situations, too. It gets back to what the Stranger says: *Takin' 'er easy.* Taking care of yourself.

BERNIE: I tell people that when stuff comes up and at a certain point it feels like it's too much, move on. It's not going anywhere and there'll be a time when you'll be ready to work with it. For now, listen to yourself. If it's not the time, don't push it. *Gently down the stream.* Some people say you have to work with everything, but there's a time and a place. If it feels like a knot, wait. It will come up again when you and the universe are ready.

JEFF: But there's also the sense of urgency, you know: *Now's the time!*

BERNIE: Now's always the time. This goes back to flowing with the grain. If there's stuff you've got to deal with and you're ready, now's the time. But if you feel like you've got to get out because you can't deal with this now, I would tell you to listen to yourself and wait. Don't cause yourself to stumble.

JEFF: Because in the long run that could deter you from finally getting where you want to go. It'll turn you off the whole process.

I think there are two streams pulling at us all the time, or at me, anyway. One is toward life and the other is toward death. The one toward life says, *Open, open, open.* I remember dropping LSD, and it was like: *Open—I'm a little uncomfortable, but . . . open, open— there's beauty here—open, open.* But I overdosed on it once, and it became: *I'm all the way open and I can't do it anymore!*

So there's opening up and there's the resistance to opening up. We're afraid that life will say, *Oh, yeah? Well, check this out. You think you can do that? Okay, let's see you.* The more you open, things just seem to get tougher and more demanding. When that happens to me, my impulse is to just say, *Fuck it. . . . Please, let it be over. Let me just be a rock, or something; I'm tired of this.* I resist giving what's needed because the need is so great. Life's asking for everything and I'm holding on.

BERNIE: And there's also our conditioning, the life we're used to. We might be in a marriage where we're beating each other up. We don't like it, we complain, but we're used to it. At the same time, something's pulling us toward a new birth, a new opening, but we don't know what it is, so we're afraid. We're torn between the unknown and the known, where we're comfortable.

JEFF: But life won't let you stay there.

BERNIE: New shit will always come to light, but it's hard to welcome something new because we have no idea what it will look like or where it's going to take us. It's not easy, but it's always growth.

JEFF: And it's sort of the only game in town, you know? Because—BOOM! We are born. What choice do we have?

BERNIE: It's the only game in town. Still, most of us won't play the game.

JEFF: To consciously play the game is wild. I remember when I first got involved with the Hunger Project over thirty years ago. Werner Erhard had these gatherings where he would talk about how enormous the problem of world hunger is, and how we know how to end it. He specified the different countries that had ended hunger and how they'd done it. It's not a problem of there not being enough food or money, or know-how, the problem is creating the political will to end it.

Then he asked the question, "What are you willing to do to create that political will? What can you do?"

He asked us not to make a gesture like donating a hundred bucks just to scratch the guilt itch, you know, to relieve ourselves of guilt, but to really do something that felt organic to our lives, something we could sustain. So I started to think about it and got really excited: *Wow! Hunger is so prevalent and at the same time so healable. And if we could end hunger, think of what confidence that would give us to address all our other deep life problems.*

I asked myself, *What are you willing to do, Jeff? Well, a guy who's involved with the media as much as you are can get the word out, meet with politicians, make movies about it.* So first I got excited in a big way, and then I started to think: *Do you really wanna do this, man? Are you sure? Are you up to it? A lot's going to be asked of you. You already have these feelings of tightness, you're not sure if you're gonna be able to pull it off. On the flip side, are you willing to go through life knowing that hunger can be ended and not do anything? Isn't that much worse?*

So I made a deal with myself. I decided to go toward the light that I could see at the end of the tunnel but if I needed to stop for a little while, that would be okay. If I was going to be asked to do something I wasn't willing to do, I wouldn't let it turn me off the entire thing, I would just take a rest for a while. This helped me go further and further, each time asking myself to do a little bit more, and then a little bit more.

That deal continued later, too, when I got involved with the End Hunger Network, along with Monte Factor, Jerry Michaud, and some others. As I suspected, I was asked to do stuff I didn't want to do. Some was too hard, too much of a reach, and I just said no. Some was just hard enough to make me stretch, like: *That's gonna be hard, man, but I'll give it a try.*

The same thing happens in other areas of my life. I do these little experiments: *I know you feel like that, but just try it and see what happens.* If it's not too far out of reach, I do it. And with each such experiment I learn something that I didn't know before. I just feel my way into it: *Whoa, this is—this is okay—I feel good. It's a stretch, and I'm feeling on purpose.*

There was that time you offered to come here with Eve to work on the book with me, and my thoughts went crazy: *I just finished this movie—I need time with Sue—I've got to have some free time—I've got to prepare for this next movie—I've got to work out—Oh, shit, they wanna come—I would love to see 'em but I wish they could do it later—They can't do it later*—I got into over-whelm, which happens to me quite often. I wish I could be a little more Dude-like. In fact, I generally find doing a movie more peaceful, because I'm completely focused. When I'm not working on a movie, the world comes rushing in.

You could tell what was happening and you said, "It's a good thing you're into Zen." That was a little koan for me, so I thought about it after we hung up. At first there was still the tightness, and then it was: *Be here in this moment. Don't torture yourself with all the shit that has to be accomplished. Where are you right now?* I relaxed a little bit, and then I thought, *Oh, Eve and Bern, yeah. It would be a chance to hang, and I could do more study with them.*

I feel the same kind of panic with making a movie. People ask me how I pick my movies. In some way I try my hardest not to pick anything, because I know what it takes when you pick what you do. Dude likes to be comfortable, man. And it seems like all the parts want me to laugh and cry and *be real* better than I did it last time. They're asking me to not be comfortable. And I say, *Come on! Been there, done that. I have to do it better or bigger? You're gonna challenge me, man?*

But what's happening is that inside I'm wondering, *Do I really have it? Can I do it?* So I resist as much as I can until a part comes along that is scarier than shit, it frightens the hell out of me, but it's too groovy to pass on. *Crazy Heart* is a perfect example. It had so many things going for it: I got to do my music, I got to be with my friends, I got to have John Goodwin write a tune. Then the voices started:

But what happens if I don't pull it off?

This is your dream. You can keep it in dreamland or make it real, your choice.

But what happens if I can't pull it off?

Yeah, but isn't this what it's all about?

And then I do it and it's better than I ever thought. Every once in a while, especially with *Crazy Heart*, *Lebowski*, or any of my favorite movies, I've got high expectations going in, and those expectations are blown out of the water because something completely more wonderful happens. There's resistance, a pushing against it, and then—BOOM! A wave breaks. But for that to happen, I have to be ready to experiment with those uncomfortable feelings. It's almost like doing yoga and stretching to touch something you can't easily reach.

I've learned to notice these reactions more and more as they happen, and instead of saying yes or no, instead of jumping in, I gently lean into the challenge a little bit. I've learned to create more space for myself; that way gives me a sense of greater freedom. And slowly, things become workable.

Cynicism is a big challenge for many people these days. I know it is for me. You say, *Oh, God, why do anything? Look at all these problems; look at these politicians. Are you kidding me? I'm not gonna vote.* So how do you work with cynicism? I guess the first step is to just notice it in you. Then begin massaging it a bit—make it workable.

Another thing I learned from all this is that my limits aren't what I think they are. In fact, each time I question them they seem to expand a little. I'm still on that same path, and my stretching gets a little bit bigger and a little bit bigger all the time. I respect my pace and at the same time I challenge it, you know? But I have to, I got to, please, befriend myself.

13.

STRIKES AND GUTTERS,

UPS AND DOWNS

JEFF: Do you experience things like that, where at first you think you've reached your limit and then, all of a sudden, it feels different and you can go on?

BERNIE: I have a slightly different take on it. Part of my training as a clown is to see how things that I perceive as failures or limits are opportunities in disguise. It reminds me of the story my clown mentor, YooWho, told me when he was doing one of his performances in a poor area in Chiapas, Mexico. At the very end of the show he announced to the big crowd in front of him, "And now, as my final glorious act, I am going to make you all disappear." And with that, he took off his glasses. He can't see without his glasses, so, of course, they all disappear. It always got a big laugh before, but not this time. All was silent, and when he put his glasses back on and looked out at the audience, he realized why. Not one person there was wearing glasses. They were too poor to wear glasses, so they couldn't get the joke.

And he had to work with that. Bearing witness to his audience and who they were, he had to find a different way to end the show.

JEFF: What did he do?

BERNIE: I don't know, I never heard that part.

JEFF: Because maybe what he did didn't work, either, and what happens then? You try to get the clown act together, you try to keep bouncing back up, and it doesn't work. I want to keep on opening and it's not working. Does that happen to you? I've talked to you about the tensions in my life, especially where I meet up with my resistance; I consider you farther down the road, but I'm curious, do you ever reach your limit? Does the clown ever stay down too long? Do you have feet of clay? If you do, show me those guys.

BERNIE: As you know, I worked with Israelis and Palestinians for a long time and finally got very frustrated. Being a Zen teacher, I know that frustrations come out of expectations, but in this case I was really attached to seeing big changes. I read Israeli and Arab newspapers every day, I followed the Palestinian news, I talked to people and tried to keep on doing things, but at some point it just felt like too much. I didn't want to go on. I didn't want to go back there, cross the checkpoints, hear the frustration in activists' voices or see the exhaustion in their eyes; I didn't want to deal with anything there anymore.

Of course, I knew this was an opportunity to open up, do more, and grow, but for several years frustration had the edge. So like you, I took a break, and now I feel different, more open to working there again. The world there has changed, not necessarily for the better, but for some reason I can feel my own energies on the rise once again.

On a more personal level, I have feet of clay like everybody else. When things feel overwhelming, my initial tendency is to run away, just get out of the scene. That's always been an issue for me. Eve and I are very different, just like you and Sue, and when our relationship feels like it's too much, my initial tendency is to get the hell out of there. So here I am, the Zen guy who's always saying that you have to deal with what is and be in the moment, and there have been lots of times in my life when I withdrew to be separate.

As I've gotten older the urge to run away has diminished, but it still comes up sometimes. Running away means not dealing with things, and that happens to me like it does for everybody else.

JEFF: The two—wanting to do things and the resistance to doing them—are so interwoven. *Fuck this, I'm not gonna do it.* That's how I deal with most tight spots, including those in my marriage to Sue. Like you with Eve, at first I get pissed: *I'm splitting. You don't get me at all; I don't get you, so fine, you go over there, I'll go over here. You do your thing and I'll do mine.* It takes a little time for the process to get moving.

I'm glad to hear that you go through this, too, that you're not a hologram or something.

BERNIE: Just this kid from Brooklyn. But in some ways I continue to look for those tough situations because I know that's how I'm going to grow. Luckily or unluckily, they keep coming up.

JEFF: I feel like my pattern of resisting began before I was born. It's an old pattern, man. Years ago I was watching TV and I heard these doctors talk about rebirthing. They said that birth is a primal kind of experience and how we reacted to it back then can teach us a lot about ourselves and our style of dealing with life. They suggested talking to your mother and asking her what your birth experience was like.

So that's what I did. Mom and I sat on chairs facing

each other, our knees almost touching, looking into each other's eyes, and she told me this: "As you know, Jeff, you had a brother, Gary, who died of sudden infant death syndrome a year before you were born. That death shook me to my core. Imagine you have a baby who's healthy and well, and one day you go over to the crib and he's not moving, he's gone. But Dr. Bellis, Leon, who delivered all you children and whom you're named after,* finally talked me into having another child and I got pregnant again. I was very excited and feeling great. When my water broke, your dad took me to the hospital, but on the way there I felt you turning, so that you were no longer in the right position to come down the birth canal, almost as if you didn't want to come out.

"When we got to the hospital, they strapped me down on one of those cold, stainless-steel tables; giving birth was different then. They gave me a spinal and also a sedative; to this day I can remember lying there while one nurse talked with another about buying a car." When she said that, I had the strangest feeling that I could remember those nurses talking.

---

* Jeff Bridges's middle name is Leon.

Then my mom went on: "But suddenly I heard one of them exclaim, 'The baby's heart stopped! Quick, get the doctor.' It turned out that I was allergic to one of the drugs they'd given me. It felt like I was falling backward down a velvet-covered escalator. Finally Leon came in and started to slap me: 'Wake up, wake up, Dorothy!' But I couldn't, because I was so drugged and strapped down. He finally told them to take the straps off me——he could tell I was trying to sit up——and right then I felt you turning back around and out you came, as if you'd changed your mind. And that's how you were born."

These doctors on TV encouraged you to take your birth experience and apply that to how you dealt with other traumatic experiences in your life. When I did that I noticed that when I'm in a tight spot I do what I did then: *No way, man, I'm digging it where I am, I don't want to be born, I'm not coming out*, and just turn around in the birth canal. It could be another movie, it could be doing something for a friend or a fan, it could be doing my hunger work, anything. Thirty-five years ago it was my marriage to Sue. I want to say, *Fuck it, I'm not gonna do that*, and get back to some safe place where nobody will bother me. But when I give myself that opportunity to say no, I find it gives me the space to say yes and to check things out after all.

I think the Dude encountered resistance, too. In fact, maybe he was kind of afraid. Maybe that's why he let go of trying to be someone or living up to something. In the movie he talks about being a radical way back in the past, but when we first meet him, the Stranger calls him the laziest man in L.A. Walter has to really egg him on to do something about that rug to get him going, and once he starts, engages, it's as if life can't leave him alone. That's what I fear, I guess.

But, as somebody said, what we're really afraid of is not how small and inadequate we are, but how big and powerful. When you think about that, it's basically saying that each of us can be Christ or Buddha; it's asking us to reach that high. But we don't want to know about that, in fact we want to protect ourselves from that knowledge. Meanwhile life is demanding that we come on, live our life.

But when it gets too intense, you have to stop.

BERNIE: You have to befriend the self.

JEFF: Give yourself a fucking break so you can move, so you can keep going. It's like yoga. I'll say, *Put your head on your fucking knees, come on!* And you know what? I get hurt because I can't do it and I'm not patient or kind to myself, I pull a muscle. I don't respect where I am. I push it too hard, I hurt myself, and that turns me off the whole process. But I could do it more gently, you know. Like, *row, row, row your boat*—gently.

Sometimes I feel that my relationship with you is a bit of a yoga pose, too. You expand faster than I want to, so it can become uncomfortable. The relationship is always about opening, jamming, digging what it is to be intimate and generous. It's asking, *Who are you? What are you?* These are the same questions that I ask myself in different situations in my life, and the challenge is not to judge myself or my answer but to just notice. One of the things that I notice is that there are limits, and limits are a cool place in which to hang.

BERNIE: Otherwise, you wind up with regrets, like you do when you hurt yourself in yoga, and you spend your energy dealing with the regrets instead of with what you originally wanted to do: *I should have done this, I shouldn't have done that.*

JEFF: *I wish I were better.*

BERNIE: It's more important to work with what happened rather than with your opinions about it. You made the best meal possible at that moment. If nobody wanted it, that's fine, you still made the best meal you were capable of. Maybe it wasn't the time for it, but that doesn't mean it won't come up again.

We make meals all the time: breakfast, lunch, dinner, snacks. We can feed ourselves and we can offer to feed people, only sometimes we waste energy on things like: *This is my meal and you've got to eat it,* or: *This is the meal I'm being served so I've got to eat it even if I don't like it.* That's another variation of *I've got to do this* or *she's got to do that,* all leading to frustration.

So if a voice says, *I should have done this,* I can say right back, *That's just your opinion, man.* It's just an opinion; there's nothing true about it. One of my Japanese Zen teachers, a famous and highly respected master, used to say, "That's a nice way of looking at it." A young, inexperienced kid would come up to him: *Hey, you're all wrong*, or *Why don't you do things this way?* Instead of telling him he's wet behind the ears and doesn't know what he's talking about, my teacher would say, "That's a nice way of looking at it."

JEFF: *That's interesting.*

BERNIE: He didn't have to prove the kid wrong, he didn't have to prove him right. It was just another opinion. We can do the same thing with the voices in our heads.

JEFF: Let's take the example of the snoring a little further. Let's say my fingers ache. What do I do? I can take Advil; I can also give myself a little injection of heroin. Where do you draw the line? Is there a line? Do you even bother to seek comfort and take an Advil for arthritis or do you abide with the pain?

BERNIE: It depends on the moment. You bear witness to your fingers aching in the same way that we bear witness to the aching of the world. In Buddhism we have something called the Middle Way. A lot of people think of that as halfway between one thing and another thing. In Zen, we say that the Middle Way is just what's happening. It's not good or bad; it's just what is. The question is, do I bear witness or not?

The fingers ache, so I might take Advil, I might not do anything, or I might take heroin. After all, they're all remedies. If I bear witness not just to the pain but also to the whole thing, the Advil might make more sense because it probably won't become an addiction like the heroin. But for someone who's already an addict and now has pain in his fingers, befriending the self might mean taking heroin.

We choose what we choose and then people have their opinions about it. Society may say, *You're screwing yourself up, you're taking heroin.* That same society sometimes tells me, *You're screwing yourself up, you're eating meat*, or *You're screwing yourself up, you're smoking a cigar.* Everybody has opinions. But if I have faith in bearing witness, if I can really just be in touch with myself, I'm going to wind up doing things that are good for me and cause me the least pain.

Having faith in yourself is what's important here, faith that you will take the actions that are appropriate for the situation at this moment.

JEFF: Yeah, more confidence. Is having faith in yourself any different from having faith in reality?

BERNIE: What's reality? I always remember Robin Williams, back when he was Mork, saying that reality is a concept.

Do I take something to relieve the pain or not? I often say about myself that I have a high tolerance level for pain and therefore pain isn't much of a problem for me. That's okay as long as I'm not attached to this thought. So I have arthritic pain. I let go of my usual concepts, get into a state of not-knowing, bear witness to the pain I feel, and then decide if I want to take something or leave it alone. I have faith in just being where I am; I'm not trapped by what happened in the past or what I expect will happen in the future. And if

I make a mistake and choose to do something that didn't work out so well, I'm not critical about what I did; I did the best I could do at that moment.

There's also the opposite approach, which is getting too arrogant. We start thinking that we can do or take care of everything. The more arrogant we become the bigger the fear that we're going to fail, that we won't live up to expectations. There are people who give the impression that they're superstars or gurus, but inside there's a nagging fear that they can't really do it all.

Going back to the tall tree that gets more wind, if you think you're some big, impervious tree that can outlast anything, you'll find yourself getting buffeted pretty badly. On the other hand, if you're just growing without worrying about whether you're big or small, then you're just blowing in the wind, you know? There's nothing extra. Stuff comes up and you bend with it.

When I did judo as a young man, I discovered that beginners can get to a place where they think they know it all, and they start looking for people they could beat. But my judo master said, "When you get into trouble, the best judo defense is to run."

The more you learn, the more you know that you're not so hot.

14.

SOME BURGERS, SOME BEERS, A FEW LAUGHS. OUR FU**ING TROUBLES ARE OVER, DUDE.

JEFF: There are a number of spiritual traditions that say that you should treat the other person as God, or divine. Turning that around, you should treat yourself the same way, and with compassion.

BERNIE: That's my opinion, too. Just don't wallow in self-pity. Take a look at the Dude. Someone pees on his rug, his home is ransacked, he's drugged and beaten up. People take advantage of him and manipulate him, but he doesn't pity himself.

JEFF: There's a difference between pity and compassion.

BERNIE: The Dude befriends himself, which is very different from wallowing in self-pity. At the end of the movie he confronts the wealthy Mr. Lebowski about how he was set up. Talking about himself, he says, "You figured, he's a loser, a deadbeat, someone the square community won't give a shit about."

Mr. Lebowski says, "Well, aren't you?"

And the Dude confesses, "Well, yeah, but . . ."

Right there he's befriending himself. He's not denying, he's not getting defensive or angry, he's not saying *How dare you!* Nor does he pity himself. He's ready to admit that he may be all those things, but there's a sense of befriending there. People knock other people because they don't see them as themselves, but we also knock ourselves and get down on a lot of things that we do. I'm for befriending them, at the same time knowing they could change.

JEFF: Sometimes I can give myself shit no matter which way I go. Was it the Dalai Lama who said that people are going to criticize you if you're this, or you're that, or even if you're right in the middle? Or was it Lincoln? I guess a lot of guys have said that. I tend to do that to myself. One day it's: *You're not pushing it hard enough, dude, you're too laid back.* Another day it's the opposite.

BERNIE: So the practice of befriending the self is a good one for you.

JEFF: Oh man, yeah. The more things I do, the more I need this compassion. When you acknowledge and see things as they are, your life feels authentic, which feels good, and those good feelings actually lead you to want to do even more, and that brings up all those voices again. On the one hand I want to do more, and on the other I don't. It's a hard choice because we affect people all the time in ways we're not even aware of, little things that have a meaning we'll never know.

I get fan letters that say, *Gee, what you've done means a lot.* Or: *You did this movie, and this one particular scene made me feel this. Please, it would mean everything to me if you'd write my son, sign something, and send it to me.* Sometimes I do it.

I mean, I'm a fan myself; I go crazy over certain guys. But how much of your time do you want to spend? On the one hand, I'm given something, I'm being acknowledged, and on the other hand I don't respond. I wish I could, or did.

There's this new thing that I'm going to try. I'm going to get a chop. You know what that is? It's one of those Chinese seals. I'll make a ceramic chop with my design and make it my official stamp. I don't know if that'll scratch the itch—it's kind of turning sour in my mouth even as I say it—because it's an awkward thing. I mean, how do you digest all that love coming at you? How do you honor the love?

I think about unrequited love, letting someone down who's asking you for something and you're not giving it. In the case of fan mail, there's too much. I can't sit down and answer it all because there are other things I want to do. But it builds up inside.

BERNIE: You know, I'm an engineer, and the first thing that comes up for me is to suggest a solution, a way out. But living with my wife, I've learned that answering the problem—

JEFF: —doesn't get it. That's right.

BERNIE: There's something else going on, and it's in the realm of emotions and feelings.

JEFF: It's not about an answer, man.

BERNIE: You could simply put on your web site: *Hey guys, I get a lot of fan mail. I love you all, but I can't answer everyone.* That's an answer. It may solve the problem, but it doesn't solve the problem in life. So when there are things that bother us, what's the real issue there? As a Zen teacher, I do one-on-one study with students. I've done this for some forty-five years, many, many times with lots of people, and the general sense I have is that people want to be heard. They don't necessarily want answers, they don't want to be told anything, they want to be heard. So the question becomes for me, can I listen? Can I acknowledge what they're saying?

JEFF: But in this case, with all the people who write me letters, I don't have the time.

BERNIE: So the issue that you're dealing with is: How do I feel good even in a situation that feels overwhelming, where I can't do everything I'd like to do? How do I feel good even in those times when I feel bad or inadequate? It's not about how you deal with all the fan mail, because you can't.

JEFF: It's like the snoring situation. Normally, I leave the room, or not answer letters. But sometimes I stay. So in this case, every once in a while, I'll take the box, read the letters, and answer. It's almost a kind of meditation.

BERNIE: You need to befriend Jeff. It's got nothing to do with the letters. You've got to befriend the fact that Jeff can only do so much.

JEFF: He does what he does.

BERNIE: And because he's famous, he's overloaded by requests. But Jeff's Jeff, he can't do everything. You can't kiss the whole world; you can only kiss so many. Sure, you could have an automatic system for answering fan mail, but the bigger issue is—

JEFF: Cutting myself slack. Don't be so un-Dude.

BERNIE: The Dude does not get angry with himself for all the things he's not doing. He befriends the self.

The number of things that we're asked to do grows as we grow, like the tree that gets more wind the taller it grows, but everybody has a limit. So the issue is cutting yourself slack.

Befriending is a beautiful thing. Don't get down, be patient. You're still going to be here the next moment, but it's going to be a whole new moment.

JEFF: I see what you're saying. You have to befriend yourself if you're going to be a Bodhisattva and work with the suffering. It's like the lenses, man. When I look with a wide lens at the whole thing and see it's all one body, you know there's nothing really wrong, but at the same time, if I look with greater magnification, I can see people suffering, including myself. The healing of both is basically the same thing. So you learn to lean into that a little bit and find your ground, at least till the next earthquake.

I can get so enthusiastic that things get overwhelming. I get into that spot with you sometimes, too. You'd like me to go on the Auschwitz retreat or do a street retreat, or else you're asking me to support your work financially. It's like you're asking, *What's up, man?*

What's the deal here? Just how generous are you? In some ways that's great, because once again, it's as if you're really asking, *Who are you? What are you?* It's an opportunity to befriend my limits and kind of surf with them a bit.

It's like when you saw the little heads I make from clay and you urged me to start the Head for Peace work right away, but I needed a little time. Sometimes I feel you're out there pulling on the grass to make it grow faster; I have a slower gestation period. I need downtime because I don't want to give in to my manic impulses. The things that I really want to nurture are slow-growing; they need space and time so that they can flower and mature.

I notice that when I'm generous, accepting, and loving toward myself, all that's reflected out into the world. The more I cut myself slack, the more I don't judge myself for not being other than I am, the more I'm aware of who I am, see it, honor it, and respect it, the more I do all those things for others. I push them less and I respect their different rhythms. You're very fast, you expand, and it's sometimes faster than I want to do it, you know? Neither one's right or wrong; it's just how it is.

I got an interesting teaching, or at least I took it

as one, from this lama from Bhutan, Khyentse Norbu Rinpoche. Alan Kozlowski told me about this lama who decided he wanted to direct movies. It's almost like the punch line of a joke, you know? *I've always wanted to direct.* Anyway, Alan said that he was coming to Santa Barbara to do a talk and would be interested in hanging out. So I went to his talk, sat up in the first row while he did his thing. I saw him kind of look at me and smile, and he said out loud, laughing a little, "You make me very nervous, sitting there looking at me." We chortled.

So I am really looking forward to hanging out with him. He has a bunch of attendants, and at the end I go up to one of them and say, "Hi, I'm Jeff Bridges, I'd like to go in and see Khyentse Norbu Rinpoche." He says, "I'll go ask." He goes in there, comes back, and says, "He doesn't want to see you." And I say, "Oh, okay." And that was the most significant teaching that he could have given me. Because one of the things that I deal with in my life is struggling with saying no, I don't have to do what everybody wants me to do.

It really lightened my load when he said no. It showed me that when someone says, *Hey, could I have your autograph?* or, *Can I take your picture?* it's okay to say, *I'll tell you what, how about a hug?* Or, *No, thanks. I love you.* Or just say, *No.*

No is beautiful. It clears the way for a *yes.* If you feel *no* and you don't express it, it just festers inside and gets expressed unskillfully. The freedom to say no, on the other hand, helps you experiment, open up a little more.

BERNIE: You're dealing with the hunger in you. You're feeding and taking care of it, so you feel better, which also makes the world around you feel better.

JEFF: [singing] *We are the world* . . .

BERNIE: That world is no other than us. When you made *Lebowski*, did you think that there would be so many people learning from the Dude? The worlds we create are way beyond anything we imagine, and the same goes for the effects we have on life. Every time we take care of some piece that we have a little resistance to—*it's going to take too much of my time, it scares me*—we become more whole, more alive. We've dealt with stuff that's been bugging us consciously or unconsciously, and it's not bugging us anymore. As we do that, we help the whole interconnected life be less bugged. Something else will come up soon, and that's okay because that's how we keep growing. We're taking care of everything, whether we're aware of it or not; it's what we call cosmic resonance. When we take care of something we think is just in us, we're affecting the whole world. With every little step we take, we're affecting everything and everyone.

Now, you talked about all the love you're getting, so let me ask you: What do you do with the hate?

JEFF: My experience is that most of the hate that comes at me comes from myself. I judge myself, *You should be, you could be*, you know.

BERNIE: I think you've got to honor that piece, too, and the best way of doing that is acknowledging: *That's your opinion, man.* You don't judge it as something bad, you don't have to call it hate or love; it's just another opinion. That's how you honor it.

15.

SAY, FRIEND, YA GOT ANY

MORE OF THAT GOOD

SARSAPARILLA?

JEFF: When I turned sixty, I read the Buddhist *Five Remembrances*. Let's see if I can remember them:

> *I am of the nature to grow old. There is no way to escape growing old.*

I am of the nature to have ill health. There is no way to escape ill health.

I am of the nature to die. There is no way to escape death.

All that is dear to me and everyone I love are of the nature to change. There is no way to escape being separated from them.

My actions are my only true belongings. I cannot escape the consequences of my actions. My actions are the ground upon which I stand.*

These *Remembrances* had a lot of resonance for me. When you're young, you feel like you're going to live forever, so you don't think about those things. Now you do. You don't let them stop you or give you the blues; they can even inspire you, if you know what I mean.

BERNIE: You're reciting some of the things that happened to Shakyamuni Buddha when he left the palace

---

* Translation by Thich Nhat Hanh as it appears in the *Plum Village Chanting Book* (Parallax Press, 1991).

grounds for the first time.* He saw somebody who was sick, someone who was old, and finally somebody who'd died, a little like what these *Remembrances* are trying to remind you. But those meetings instilled some deep questions in him: *What's at the bottom of all of this? What's this life about?* I don't know if that's what happened to you. Realizing you're going to die can give you the freedom to be born again.

JEFF: There's a little guy inside saying, *You're going to kick outta here pretty soon. You wanna do some stuff, and what you do will have consequences.* Consequences are a kind of immortality. All the things that you love are going to change; you're going to lose them one way or another.

BERNIE: It makes them all of a sudden very dear.

---

* This relates to the story surrounding the life of Gautama Shakyamuni, who was later called the Buddha, the Awakened One.

JEFF: Not only the things you love, but also the things you don't love, because you know they're going to go, too. *I'm of the nature that I'll get sick.* I can feel my health going in a gentle kind of way, but it doesn't bum me out so much. If I was younger, I think I would have reacted differently.

BERNIE: *I'm of the nature that I will die.* Imagine really grokking that when you're younger. Imagine if we could live our whole life that way: *Hey, I'm going to die, so let's live! The things I'm surrounded by are going to change and disappear, so let me enjoy their beauty as they are right now.*

JEFF: Remembering that the stuff that we do has ramifications and that everything is connected.

BERNIE: The word *karma* has entered our Western vocabulary. It means that everything has consequences. That implies that everything is interconnected. Touch a little thing and it ripples throughout the universe, it affects everything.

JEFF: I'm older and I'm open to scaling down, selling the house we live in now and getting something smaller. There's something great about that, but it also means that the game is kind of over. I sense these two impulses. One says, *Do, do, do, achieve, achieve, achieve.* The other says, *Sssshhhh, please relax. Do you want to spend the rest of your life doing some sort of never-ending homework assignment? Sssshhhh . . .*

There's a tale I relate to that goes back to Greek mythology, about the nymph Daphne, whom the god Apollo falls in love with. She doesn't want him and runs away, but Apollo keeps coming: *You don't understand who I am, baby. I am the guy who's the king of all art, medicine, poetry, and all that stuff; you don't know what you're missing.* But she doesn't want all that, it's too intense for her, so she goes to her father and says, *Dad, here's the deal. This god wants me. He's coming after me, talking about all this stuff and all this drama, but I just don't want it, you know, it's too much, I want simplicity. Look at that beautiful tree, it doesn't have to worry about any of this. There's nothing extra, no separation anywhere, it's just a tree.* And her father, a demigod himself, says, "Fine," and turns her into a laurel tree.

Working on my movies, getting married, having

kids, doing my music—that's the stuff Apollo talks about. At some point you start cutting down to live simpler. You've done your thing, it's getting time to die. Every time you take a large step, like marriage, it takes you closer to that last step. And I notice that I'm feeling this sense of *Come on, realize all the things you want to realize, because pretty soon you won't be here, so do it now.*

I'm in the process of writing a song. I do it like I do the little heads, I don't think too much about the words, they just come out and then I wonder what they mean. I remember meeting the artist Mayumi Oda at your Symposium for Western Socially Engaged Buddhism. I looked at her gorgeous prints and asked her, "How do you do this?" And her answer was, "It's like I'm already dead."

I relate to that in a big way. It's not like *I know I'm gonna die*, which is the hopeless, rote way of looking at it, like *Nobody gets out of here alive.* I think what she meant was that it gives her a place to act from, a carefreeness that maybe she didn't have before. You're going to go anyway, so you no longer have to be afraid of failing or what people think about you, or any of that. I noticed that with my mom and other people who got old. You're getting there yourself, how old are you now?

BERNIE: I'm young, I'm seventy-three.

JEFF: You're a baby, man. But older folks like my mom didn't give a shit. There was no time for mincing any words, just: *This is it*. And there's something beautiful and kind of relaxing about that.

Here's the song I'm working on:

> *I'm living like I'm already dead.*
> *Like I've said what I've said.*
> *Like I am what I am.*
> *Like Popeye and my mom,*
> *Like my dad and this song.*
> *I'm gone, and here I come again.*
> *I'm living like I'm already dead.*
> *Juggling diamonds and lead.*
> *Jumping over the sky.*
> *And I don't care if I can sift through all this sand.*
> *Cuz I'm gone, and here I come again.*
> *I'm living like I'm already dead.*
> *Turning black and white to red.*
> *My kids know that I love 'em.*
> *And I've done what I do.*

Magically, I found you.
I'm gone, and here I come again.

I don't know where I'm going with it. It conjures up a feeling of being here and not being here, so you might as well do what you need to do.

Gone, gone, gone. How does that go?

BERNIE: *Gaté, Gaté, Paragaté, Parasamgaté.* It's a mantra at the end of the *Heart Sutra. Gone, gone, completely gone, gone beyond.*

JEFF: What is that about?

BERNIE: It means *gone to the other shore.* But again, the other shore is right under our feet, so it's back to: *Row, row, row your boat.*

JEFF: Live your life, only this time live it as if you're gone or not there, as if you're already dead.

BERNIE: In Zen, when we push people to realize the state of not knowing, completely letting go, we'll use phrases like *You've got to kill yourself*, or *You've got to die on the cushion*. What we really mean is that you have to get into the state of *The Dude is not in*. It's a little like you say, live as if you're gone, live without attachment to who or what Jeff is. But at the very instant that you die you must get reborn in order to do things. That could be what you were alluding to when you talked about your mother, who had no patience for nonsense anymore. You do things as if you're already dead, which means that you can do a lot. In some way, that can really empower you to be whatever you want to be.

You could have also done that much earlier in your life, say at the age of five: *Man, I've lived a whole five years. I've lived my life, and now I can do whatever I want.* You could do that at the age of twenty: *I've lived a whole twenty years; I've lived my life and now I can do what I want.* You can live your life like that whenever you wish; you don't have to wait till you get old.

JEFF: What is living your life? Is it doing what you want?

BERNIE: For me, it's doing what comes up, like the jazz band. It's not just you or me, and it's not just everybody else, it's the vibe of the whole scene. But you're your main instrument and you're doing your thing completely. You're not thinking twice, you're not saying, *Hey, I shouldn't play this riff* or *I gotta think about it.* You're jamming. Things happen, life happens, and you're jamming.

JEFF: You get in the zone and you're gone, but something's coming through you somehow.

But all this is just our opinion, man.

BERNIE: Exactly, it's just our opinion.

JEFF: This is fun, Bern. Enjoyed the hang.

BERNIE: So, Jeff, do you think we've been rowing our boat merrily down the stream?

JEFF: Can't help but, Bernsky.

BERNIE: We haven't gotten into any fistfights.

JEFF: No, no.

BERNIE: Or stuff like that. It's been great jamming with you.

JEFF: I'll say. [singing] *Row, row, row your boat, gently down the stream.*

BERNIE: [singing with Jeff] *Merrily, merrily, merrily, merrily. Life is but a dream.*

JEFF: Now let's do it as a round. You start.

BERNIE: *Row, row, row your boat.* [in a round]

JEFF: *Row, row, row your boat.* [laughter] I fucked up! [laughter] *Life is but a dream!* [laughter]

BERNIE: That was great. Let's do it again sometime.

JEFF: Yeah.

ACKNOWLEDGMENTS

BERNIE: It was fun hanging, but it seems like there were a lot of other folks also hanging around to make this happen.

JEFF: Yeah, I'm feeling a bunch of gratitude bubbling up. First, to the Brothers. They created the whole thing. Before we started this project, I gave Joel Coen a call and asked him if it would be okay with him and Ethan for us to do this. I wanted to make sure that we weren't pissing on their turf and that they knew what we were

up to, and he said go for it. He gave us their blessing.
Without that I wouldn't have done this.

And what about our lady friends?

BERNIE: Yeah man, our partners.

JEFF: Your lady friend, Eve, really pulled all our
words together to make a book out of them. You know,
in music, all the musicians get together to make their
music, but they need a producer to make sense out of it
all, and that's what Evie did for us.

BERNIE: And where would you be without Sue, man?
She's prominent not only in this book but in your whole
life. She gives you the space to be where you want to be
and do what you want to do.

JEFF: Yeah, keeping to the whole "rowing your boat"
metaphor, without her I'd be up the creek without a
paddle.

And speaking of family, I got to thank my brother
Beau, sister Cindy, daughters Isabelle, Jessie, and Hay-
ley, my parents, everyone in my family—living and
dead—who're still holding me.

BERNIE: I want to really say thank you to Alan Koz-lowski for being such an important part of the hang in Montana. He wired us for sound and took some amazing photos. And don't forget the wonderful team you got working with you.

JEFF: How can I forget? David Schiff, Bob Wallerstien, Jean Sievers, Becky Pedretti, and my daughter Jessie, who's been my assistant on the last three movies. And what about your team, Bern?

BERNIE: Ike Eichenlub, the great Dudist fact-checker, made sure we got that brilliant dialogue straight. And Peter Cunningham, who's photographed me on my journeys for over thirty years, did the same for this book journey. And we were lucky to work with David Rosenthal and Sarah Hochman at Blue Rider Press!

JEFF: They had the faith, stupidity, and patience to work with us.

BERNIE: I deeply appreciate my teachers, not just in Zen but also in the world of math, who encouraged me to take all this esoteric stuff and put it into street language. Nobody better than the Dude for that. And I especially have to thank Yogi Berra, Groucho Marx, and Lenny Bruce for their help with my koan practice.

JEFF: And to Billy Shore and Jerry Michaud, who continue holding the torch to end hunger in our country, and—you know, Bern, we got to thank the whole world!

BERNIE: Yeah, we got to attach the *Encyclopaedia Britannica* to this page.

JEFF: Not just everyone who's ever lived but also all the people who haven't been born yet, because they're kind of pulling us along, you know?

BERNIE: And also to those who will never be born. Hey Jeff, let's go bowling.

JEFF: Nah, let's go smoke a cigar.